BrightRED Study Guide

Curriculum for Excellence

N5

ENGLISH

Dr Christopher Nicol

BrightRED
PUBLISHING

First published in 2013 by:
Bright Red Publishing Ltd
1 Torphichen Street
Edinburgh
EH3 8HX

A CIP record for this book is available from the British Library

ISBN 978-1-906736-36-1

With thanks to:
PDQ Digital Media Solutions Ltd (layout) and Ivor Normand (copy-edit and proof-read)

Cover design and series book design by Caleb Rutherford – e i d e t i c

Acknowledgements
Every effort has been made to seek all copyright holders. If any have been overlooked, then Bright Red Publishing will be delighted to make the necessary arrangements.

Alexander Raths/Shutterstock.com (p6); Pressmaster/Shutterstock.com (p8); Sergii Figurnyi/Shutterstock.com (p8); Cheryl Savan/Shutterstock.com (p9); Robert Kneschke/Shutterstock.com (p9); AlexandreNunes/Shutterstock.com (p9); mast3r/Shutterstock.com (p9); Jeka/Shutterstock.com (p9); Vibrant Image Studio/Shutterstock.com (p9); grafvision/Shutterstock.com (p11); photomak/Shutterstock.com (p11); The poem 'Still I Rise', taken from the book 'And Still I Rise' by Maya Angelou, published by Virago, an imprint of Little, Brown Book Group (p12); 'Strange Fruit' music and words by Lewis Allan – © 1939 – EDWARD B MARKS MUSIC COMPANY – Copyright renewed; extended term of copyright derived from Lewis Allan assigned and effective July 21, 1995 to MUSIC SALES CORPORATION – all rights for the world outside of USA controlled by EDWARD B MARKS MUSIC COMPANY – All Rights Reserved – Used by kind permission of Carlin Music Corp., London NW1 8BD (p12); Sanja Gjenero (p14); An extract from the article 'Not so good to talk: mobile calls fall for first time since 90s' by John Plunkett, taken from The Guardian, 18th July 2012. Copyright Guardian News & Media Ltd 2012 (p15); Talk is cheap, but texting is cheaper' by Lisa Markwell taken from 'The Independent' 19th July 2012 © The Independent (p15); Illustration © The 2D Workshop (pp16-17); A graph based on the research of: Adler, R., Rosenfeld, L. and Proctor, R. (2001) 'Interplay: the process of interpersonal communicating', Fort Worth, TX: Harcourt © skillsyouneed.com (p18); CREATISTA/Shutterstock.com (p18); bzuko22 (p19); bzuko22 (p19); wavebreakmedia/Shutterstock.com (p20); wuestenigel (p22); sergign/Shutterstock.com (p24); Brian A Jackson/Shutterstock.com (p26); NADIIA IEROKHINA/Shutterstock.com (p27); An extract from the article 'Red hair is a beacon in a sea of mediocrity', by Rosemary Goring, taken from 'The Herald', Monday 2nd July 2012 © Herald & Times Group (p29); bzuko22 (p29); bzuko22 (p29); Claudia Meyer (p29); Jeka/Shutterstock.com (p30); len-k-a (p30); funkyfrogstock/Shutterstock.com (p30); len-k-a (p31); Vanessa Zanini Fernandes (p31); Brendan Howard/Shutterstock.com (p31); Wanchai Orsuk/Shutterstock.com (p32); An extract from the article 'How to survive in the age of distraction' by Johann Hari, taken from 'The Independent' June 24th 2011 © The Independent (p34); An extract from the article 'The Passion of the Morrissey' by Chloe Veltman taken from 'The Believer' July-August 2012 Music Issue © Chloe Veltman (p34); An extract from the article 'Cycling Scotland's new Hebridean Trail' by Jonathan Thompson, taken from 'The Guardian' 01 September 2012. Copyright Guardian News & Media Ltd 2012 (p35); Hans Gruber/Shutterstock.com (p36); An extract from 'Why you can never look good in a fur coat' by Hadley Freeman, taken from 'The Guardian' 07 February 2011. Copyright Guardian News & Media Ltd 2012 (p36); Elnur/Shutterstock.com (p36); Ronan Crowley/Creative Commons (CC BY-ND 2.0)[1] (p37); An extract from the article 'Paradise Found' by Paddy Woodworth, taken from 'The Irish Times', September 1st, 2012 © Paddy Woodworth (p37); wavebreakmedia/Shutterstock.com (p39); magicinfoto/Shutterstock.com (p40); Monkey Business Images/Shutterstock.com (p42); Daniel_Dash/Shutterstock.com (p43); Joyce Vincent/Shutterstock.com (p44); Pavel L Photo and Video/Shutterstock.com (p47); David Hughes/Shutterstock.com (p48); An extract from the article 'Bowie ballyhoo that's enough to make a laughing gnome weep!' by Jan Moir. Originally published in: Daily Mail 11/01/2013 © Daily Mail (p49); An extract from 'Michael Morpurgo interview' by Hermione Hoby, from 'The Daily Telegraph' 30 May 2011 © Telegraph Media Group Limited 2011 (p50); Tim Duncan/Creative Commons (CC BY 3.0)[2] (p51); Sanja Gjenero (p53); Image taken from 'The Strange Case of Dr Jekyll and Mr Hyde: A Graphic Novel' by Robert Louis Stevenson (Author), Alan Grant (Editor), Cam Kennedy (Illustrator), published by Waverley Books Ltd; First edition (21 Feb 2008) © DC Thomson books (p54); Chris Dorney/123rf (p56); ronstik/Shutterstock.com (p58); Andy Dean Photography/Shutterstock.com (p59); RTimages/Shutterstock.com (p61); Davide Guglielmo (p62); bzuko22 (p63); bzuko22 (p63); Extracts from 'The Strange Case of Dr Jekyll and Mr Hyde: A Graphic Novel' by Robert Louis Stevenson (Author), adapted by Alan Grant, Cam Kennedy (Illustrator) Waverley Books Ltd; First edition (21 Feb 2008) © DC Thomson books (pp64-5); An extract from the poem 'Retrieving and Renewing. A poem for ASLS', by Edwin Morgan, 2004, http://www.arts.gla.ac.uk/ScotLit/ASLS/ (p66); Photo © Alan Riach (p66); An extract from 'A Drunk Man Looks at the Thistle', published by Blackwood (Edinburgh, Scotland), 1926 (p67); marekuliasz/Shutterstock.com (p68); Kamil Porembinski/Creative Commons (CC BY-SA 2.0)[3] (p69); Elnur/Shutterstock.com (p69); Photo © Independent Talent Group Ltd (p70); A photo from the Matrix Theatre Company production of Bold Girls taken from http://www.matrixtheatre.com/shows/boldgirls.html © Matrix Theatre Company (p73); An extract from 'Bold Girls' by Rona Munro, published by Hodder Gibson, 1995. Reproduced by permission of Hodder Education (pp74-5); Photograph by Eileen Heraghty/7:84. Reprinted by permission of the Trustees of the National Library of Scotland (p77); Photo © Petra Liebetanz (p79); Photo © Canongate Books (p80); (p); Photo take from www.glasgowguide.co.uk © Martin Smith (p82); An extract from 'Away in a Manger' by Anne Donovan, taken from 'Hieroglyphics And Other Stories'. Published by Canongate Books 2004. Reproduced by permision of Canongate Books Ltd. (p82-3); The book cover of 'Hieroglyphics And Other Stories' by Anne Donovan © Canongate Books Ltd. (p84); Photo © Claudia Kraszkiewicz (p86); An extract from 'Hyena' by Edwin Morgan. Taken from 'Collected Poems' (Carcanet Press, 1990), copyright © Edwin Morgan 1990 (p87); An extract from 'In the Snack-bar' by Edwin Morgan. Taken from Collected Poems (Carcanet Press, 1990), copyright © Edwin Morgan 1990 (p87); Book cover © Mariscat Press (p88); The poem 'Tithonus' by Alfred Tennyson, 1833 (public domain) (p89); The poem 'Good Friday' by Edwin Morgan. Taken from Collected Poems (Carcanet Press, 1990), copyright © Edwin Morgan 1990 (p90); Thomas Nugent/Creative Commons (CC BY-SA 2.0)[3] (p91); Thomas Nugent/Creative Commons (CC BY-SA 2.0)[3] (p94); Lucky Business/Shutterstock.com (p96); eelnosiva/Shutterstock.com (p99); dotshock/Shutterstock.com (p101); Aniblo (p101); Leroy Skalstad (p101); Sanja Gjenero (p101); An extract from 'A Chitterin Bite' by Anne Donovan, taken from 'Hieroglyphics And Other Stories'. Published by Canongate Books 2004. Reproduced by permision of Canongate Books Ltd. (p82-3); Stefan Wagner, trumpkin.de (p102); Zurijeta/Shutterstock.com (p103); An extract from 'Black & Blue' by Ian Rankin, published by Orion Books Ltd 1997 (p104); An extract from 'The Cutting Room' by Louise Welsh, published by Canongate Books Ltd 2002 (p104); Korionov/Shutterstock.com (p105); Iancu Cristian/Shutterstock.com (p106); maga/Shutterstock.com (p107); Andi Collington (p108); Iablonskyi Mykola/Shutterstock.com (p109); Ned Horton (http://www.HortonGroup.com) (p109); Jelle Boontje (p109); Emilian Robert Vicol/Creative Commons (CC BY 2.0)[4] (p111); Calin Tatu/Shutterstock.com (p112); Wallenrock/Shutterstock.com (p115); The closing section of Ed Milliband's speech to his party conference in 2012. Reproduced with permission of The Labour Party (p115); Cartoon by Mac [Stan McMurtry]: 'Good news, George. Apparently our gas bills might be a few pence cheaper'. Originally published in: Daily Mail 14/12/2012 © Associated Newspapers Limited (p117); Giuseppe_RShutterstock.com (p120); Seth Sawyers/Creative Commons (CC BY 2.0)[4] (p122); bzuko22 (p123); bzuko22 (p123); Erin English/Creative Commons (CC BY-ND 2.0)[1] (p125).

[1](CC BY-ND 2.0) http://creativecommons.org/licenses/by-nd/2.0/
[2](CC BY 3.0) http://creativecommons.org/licenses/by/3.0/
[3](CC BY-SA 2.0) http://creativecommons.org/licenses/by-sa/2.0/
[4](CC BY 2.0) http://creativecommons.org/licenses/by/2.0/

Printed and bound in the UK, by Martins the Printers.

CONTENTS

INTRODUCING NATIONAL 5 ENGLISH

As the world becomes more and more of a global village, the challenges for making your mark in it are becoming ever more demanding. In the upcoming decades of your working life, you will face competition from all over the globe. This makes the future much more exciting. It's a future, however, for whose changes you need to be thoroughly well prepared.

It will not be enough simply to be highly knowledgeable about your chosen activity or profession; you will also need to be able to project your character and personality in a way that maximises your chances of success in the world in which you find yourself. That's where National 5 comes in.

THE BENEFITS OF NATIONAL 5

This is a course which allows you opportunities to develop and extend a wide range of language-focused life skills.

These skills include enhanced communication abilities to ensure that you can operate successfully in group interchanges and team working. In addition, your capacity to present your own ideas and to interpret the aims and intentions of others will be enriched. Your critical thinking and conceptualising skills will be significantly extended as you learn how to listen, talk, read and write in ways that are appropriate to the many contexts and tasks with which you will be confronted throughout your working life.

It's a well-grounded way of tackling the world of work, one which puts you in charge of your life. It's an empowering fusion of language and life skills to carry you forward successfully.

There's quite a lot to come to terms with in this course – but, broken down as it will be here, the structure is fairly straightforward. So, what actually is the structure?

THE EXTERNAL ASSESSMENT

At the course's end, you will be assessed externally by two components:

Component 1 – The Exam

This is made up of a question paper in which:

- 30 marks will be allocated to a Close Reading exercise on a non-fiction text

- 20 marks will be allocated to the production of a critical essay on a text which you will have studied in class

- 20 marks will be allocated to answering questions on a short extract from a Scottish fiction text which you will have studied in class, and you will also be asked to relate aspects of the extract to ideas and/or **themes** that you have noticed elsewhere in the work(s) you have studied.

Component 2 – The Portfolio

This is a portfolio incorporating two pieces of writing in different **genres**: one broadly creative, the other broadly discursive. 15 marks will be awarded for each of these.

In total, Component 1 accounts for 70% of the total mark and Component 2 accounts for 30%. Your final grade will be determined by your performance in these two components.

THE MANDATORY UNITS

In addition, however, you will be assessed by your school on two Units which you will be required to pass in order to achieve the overall award.

The two units which make up the National 5 course are:

- Analysis and Evaluation
- Creation and Production

You'll learn more about these in the 'Tackling the Units' chapter and you can refer to page 126 at the back of this guide for a breakdown of how the Units operate.

So, those are the Units. Now let's look at how best to tackle them.

HOW WILL THIS GUIDE HELP YOU MEET THE CHALLENGES?

This guide has one priority: your success. We 're here to help you meet the multiple challenges of the course. And we promise we'll be talking **to** you and not **at** you at all times!

So let's look at the challenges.

Spoken Interaction

Both Units foreground Spoken Interaction in Outcome 2 of each one. We will take you through all the skills required here: what to say, how to say it, how to discern aims and purposes, how to read non-verbal signals as you watch and listen to speakers. We'll suggest how the knowledge and research you acquire here can be redirected into essay format later should you so wish.

Reading for Understanding, Analysis and Evaluation

Commonly known as Close Reading, this competence will account for 30% of your final external assessment and will also play its part in Outcome 1 of the Analysis and Evaluation Unit. We'll also suggest how the techniques learned here can enrich your Folio writing.

Critical Essay

How to go about reading and interpreting the questions, how to plan, how to structure your introduction, body paragraphs and conclusions, how to deal with quotations: all these are set out carefully so that your enjoyment of the text can be translated into examination success.

The Folio

The Folio offers you a wide range of writing possibilities to choose from. We'll talk you through the issues to consider before making your choice and offer 'hands-on' advice for success in the various genres.

Scottish Context Work

Many of the analytical skills you acquired earlier in this guide will again stand you in good stead here. You'll also learn how to deal with the new challenges it sets up when you need to relate certain passages to other works by the same author or other sections of the text.

So, there you have it. National 5 in easy stages. In addition, we provide you with tips and techniques for getting round various problems as they arise in our 'Don't Forget' and 'Things to Do and Think About' text boxes. There will also be online activities to allow you to check on your progress.

So, let's get started.

ONLINE

This book is supported by the BrightRED Digital Zone – log on at www.brightredbooks.net/N5English to unlock a world of tests, videos, games and more.

TACKLING THE UNITS: AN INTEGRATED APPROACH

YOUR NATIONAL 5 UNITS

One of the most helpful features of your National 5 course is that your performance for the Units can be assessed in a variety of ways. Success no longer depends solely on your reading and writing skills. Into the picture now come your talking and listening abilities, to help assessors determine much more fully your true performance in carrying out various tasks in English.

WHAT WILL I LEARN HERE?

This broader assessment of your abilities provides a host of interesting ways to establish your credentials in these Units. Happily, the possibilities for assessment through spoken interaction allow you opportunities to practise and develop your talking, listening, reading and writing skills in a way that integrates them as much as you may wish. Obviously, we have to look at talking and listening tactics in close detail: how to prepare for group discussion, how to function in group interaction, how to listen productively, how to listen for a speaker's intentions and how to determine success. But this is not the end of the story.

From your preparations for talking and listening, you will acquire valuable material which can be used in other ways. Your skills in analysing and evaluating research material for these interactions will be significantly developed – and this material, in turn, can extend and enrich your essay-writing opportunities. This will prove valuable, not only for Unit assessments but also for Folio work.

We will use this chapter, then, not only to develop talking and listening skills but also to expand them to offer you opportunities for enhancing your reading and writing capabilities. At the end of this section, you will find our 'Outcomes Check' section. This will allow you to see just how the evidence you have generated matches up to the SQA's success criteria for these Units.

But first, let's get started by talking about group discussion and its place in your skills development.

THE IMPORTANCE OF DISCUSSION

The world revolves around talking. Just think how much time we spend in a day talking to our family, to our friends, to our teachers and to the casual contacts we meet in our daily lives. Sometimes we talk in one-to-one situations, sometimes in small groups.

We can find ourselves discussing a whole host of subjects: burning issues of the day, aspects of the courses we study, problems we find ourselves facing, choices needing to be made. Some will affect our personal lives, others our education, others still our jobs and the communities in which we live. The ability to interact successfully with others in group discussions is a vital life skill which brings us a variety of benefits and advantages. So, let's take a closer look at what's involved in successful **interaction** in your National 5 course, and in your life well beyond that.

WHAT ARE THE BENEFITS?

The result of participating regularly in group **discussions** is that we learn how to put forward our views confidently – and persuasively. We learn how to contribute effectively to any exchange of views we encounter.

In a school or college environment, group discussions may add depth to our study of a topic or teach us how to win agreement in a debate. In the world of work, mastery of the tools of group discussion will help us in problem-solving and decision-making.

Group-discussion expertise will assist us in becoming progressively more articulate and thereby more successful in advancing our opinions in whatever sphere we find ourselves.

Interacting with others in discussions allows us to get a sharper perspective on topics of importance to us. Listening to other people's views helps us to deepen our own. By discussion, we get a better all-round picture of an issue. Understanding is improved and tolerance promoted.

WHAT EXACTLY IS A GROUP DISCUSSION?

Put simply, a group discussion is any situation in which a number of participants exchange information and opinions on a given topic, problem or issue. In this exchange of views, agreement may or may not be achieved, but each member has an obligation to make a significant contribution in helping add depth to the deliberations.

Each member must approach the group with an open mind, genuinely prepared to listen as well as to argue his or her point of view. In a good group discussion, you will probably hear views with which you strongly disagree – but you must respect your opponent's point of view and his or her right to hold it ... if, that is, you expect your own opinions to be accorded the same courtesy.

WHAT ARE THE ORAL SKILLS REQUIRED?

A good group discussion involves much more than deploying good oral skills. But let's look first at the kind of language you might find helpful in putting forward your case.

- Be **concise**. Other people are waiting to take part. Make your case fully but avoid being too long-winded. Don't hog the discussion!

- Be **clear**. Clear expression is a sign of clear thinking. Avoid complicated sentences which will lose the attention of your fellow participants. Present ideas in a logical order which is easy to follow.

- Be **natural**. Remember you are talking **to** people, not **at** them. Anything which sounds rehearsed sounds stilted, false and generally unconvincing. Cultivate a natural-sounding delivery in straightforward language. If you have an accent, be proud of it. It is part of you.

- Be **positive**. Present, where you can, the benefits/advantages of your viewpoint rather than insist on the shortcomings/disadvantages of your opponent's. When you need to disagree, do so politely in unaggressive language.

- Be **persuasive**. Be careful not to sound threatening in your approach to the topic. Use language with which others can agree. Remember, you are seeking support for your views. Win them over with your reasonable-sounding, considered stance.

- Be **reactive**. Don't be shy about picking up a point made by someone else and asking them to explain it further. Seeking clarification is an excellent way of moving a discussion onward. React, too, to the level of formality of the discussion. Sometimes, practice discussions might be fairly informal affairs; at other times, you will need to adopt a more formal **tone** for more serious assessment discussions.

ONLINE TEST

Check what you already know about group discussions by testing yourself online, at www. brightredbooks.net/N5English

DON'T FORGET

A successful group discussion should leave all participants feeling that they have contributed meaningfully to a full and balanced exploration of a subject.

DON'T FORGET

A good discussion will often find you getting emotionally involved. But don't lose your temper over views with which you disagree or with the people putting them forward. Keep your language calm if you wish first to win and then to retain the support of neutral members of the group. Nobody likes Mr Angry!

THINGS TO DO AND THINK ABOUT

Think about and discuss with a partner how successful, or otherwise, you find the following extracts from a group discussion. Be prepared to say why you feel that the contributions are effective or not. Use the above guidelines to help you evaluate.

'I hear what you are saying, but surely discussing colour is not necessarily a sign of being a racist?'

'It's not that I'm against this war, it's just that it's difficult to support something which is, well, like killing innocent people where life is difficult, what with the famine ... and stuff, like.'

'I understand your point, and while I agree to a certain extent, I can't go along with your claim that exams are a total waste of time. For a start, they ...'

'What I like about the film is its life-enhancing view of humanity, which is uplifting and at the same time penetrating in its attitude towards life.

'Listen! You've totally misunderstood what the book is about. How wrong can you be?!'

THE ROLE OF BODY LANGUAGE

A successful group discussion is not just about **what** you say; it is also about **how** you say it. You need to show yourself as being part of a group as well as part of a discussion. That means being as aware of your body language as of your oral input. For instance, what signal does slouching back in your chair send out? Or stabbing your finger in the air to make a point?

SUCCESSFUL GROUP DISCUSSION

One researcher has suggested that between 60 and 70 per cent of all meaning is derived from non-verbal behaviour. Clearly, how you sit and behave in the course of the discussion matters, so we'll take a look at what body language adds to group discussions.

- **Body posture.** Find a comfortable position to sit in, one which suggests interest and alert but relaxed engagement in the discussion. Slumping back in your chair might suggest boredom; leaning too far forward might suggest aggression.

- **Eye contact.** Engage with the group as a whole. Fixing your attention on any one member might suggest lack of confidence; looking around the group reassures members that you are addressing them all and that you value everyone's opinion.

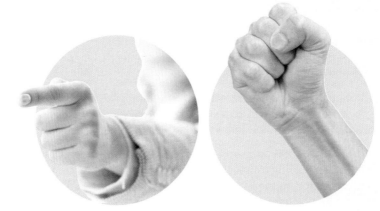

- **Hand gestures.** Many people find it natural to express themselves with hand movements as well as words. This is not a problem here unless the gestures hint at aggression: finger-pointing or table-thumping, for example, or if they become distracting and irritating to the group.

A successful discussion requires the full cooperation of the group at every level. Everyone must be prepared to talk, to listen, to show their involvement, to respect the opinions of others and to keep the flow of discussion moving to ensure that, at its completion, the discussion has enriched everyone's knowledge and understanding of the topic.

Easily said, but how do we go about ensuring that all this happens? One way is to think about the **organisation** of the group. So, that's what we'll look at in the next section.

THINGS TO DO AND THINK ABOUT

Here are two tasks which will help you to evaluate the importance of body language in a group discussion:

Task 1

Study with a partner these participants in a group discussion and suggest what their body language or facial expressions signal. Say how well or badly you consider them to be performing in a group discussion, giving your reasons.

Task 2

Form yourselves into groups of four or five. Consider this:

You have been stranded on a desert island. What three items would you want to have with you? Take a few minutes to make notes before starting.

When you finish, get a member of the group to report back to the rest of the class on what you decided.

How well did you get on with your discussion? Check out these areas and award your group a grade.

	Really well	Satisfactory	Could have been much better
Avoided awkward pauses			
Balanced group participation			
Kept to task			
Group harmony			
Body language			

So, how did it go? Did the discussion flow, or were there awkward pauses? Did everyone contribute in equal measure? Did anyone wander off topic? How well did the group get on? Was body language used to best advantage? How good a job was done by the person reporting?

DON'T FORGET

Be sure to put into practice all that you have learned about oral skills and body language.

HOW TO GET THE BEST OUT OF OUR GROUP?

One way is to allocate roles to the various group members so that, once we know our role, we can intervene appropriately. What might these roles be?

DON'T FORGET ➕

Over the course of the term, it is a good idea to rotate the roles of chairperson and reporter around all members of the group so that everyone gets the benefit of developing these important life skills.

DON'T FORGET ➕

Criticise an idea, by all means, but don't attack the person putting it forward. Use reason, not emotion, to show up what you think are the shortcomings of the idea or argument.

THE CHAIRPERSON

The chairperson or leader will:

- introduce the topic and suggest what form the discussion will take
- invite each member of the group to participate in turn
- ensure that the group remains on task/topic
- ensure a balanced discussion, encouraging quieter members to talk and discouraging any individual member from dominating the discussion
- intervene when conflict threatens between members

THE REPORTER

The reporter or recorder will:

- make notes of the key points made during the discussion
- summarise the outcome, outlining any divisions of opinion which emerged
- report back to the class on the findings of the group

THE INDIVIDUAL MEMBER

Each individual group member will:

- provide personal, relevant and substantial ideas/opinions/experiences
- take account of what others have to say, show support, raise questions or doubts and seek clarification when necessary
- make notes on points which might be raised later as a result of the contribution of others
- avoid interrupting the contributions of others until they are complete

TEAM-BUILDING TALK

A good group discussion will often arouse strong feelings in the participants. Open conflict, however, is the enemy of progress in a discussion. Good group-discussion manners require us all to choose our language carefully and to think of the feelings of others when we formulate our comments. That doesn't mean you avoid making your point strongly; you just do it in a way that doesn't upset the atmosphere in the group. This means that the debate doesn't hit a brick wall of hostility.

Here are some **DO**s and **DON'T**s of discussion language.

Don't say!	Do say!
That's a load of tripe!	*I'm not quite with you. Could you maybe give us some specific examples?*
You're off your head!	*Maybe I'm being a bit slow, but I'm not following you. A bit of evidence might help.*
You've gone on long enough! Give other folk a chance!	*Time's running on. Maybe someone else would like to come in here?*
For heaven's sake, Christine, you must have something to say!	*Christine, you're a bit quiet there. Would you agree with Mike on that point?*
I'm bored! Hasn't this gone on long enough?	*Since we only have a few minutes left, maybe we should get on to the next point?*
This is doing my head in! Just what are we on about here?	*Am I the only one who's a bit lost here? Maybe we need to get back to the original question?*
And what's that supposed to mean, eh?	*I think I see what you're getting at, but a few more details would help.*

Everything we've said here is about creating an atmosphere in which profitable discussion can flourish. Respecting these simple guidelines can create an environment where everyone is included, where everyone is respected and where everyone's opinion is valued. In this way, discussion progresses, knowledge is enriched and understanding increases. A good discussion, a commentator once remarked, should generate more light than heat. Be careful to ensure that your discussions do just that: create helpful enlightenment, not pointless hot air.

ONLINE

Much of what we have been saying here applies to the academic world in which you currently find yourselves. For a perspective on group discussion in the world of work; check out the 'Group discussions' link at www.brightredbooks.net/N5English. Scroll down to the bottom of the page, and you will find no fewer than 17 different sections on this topic!

THINGS TO DO AND THINK ABOUT

Imagine you are taking on the role of chairperson in a group discussion on the topic of cloning. How will you introduce the topic? How will you ensure that each group member participates? What sort of language will you use to defuse any conflicts which may emerge?

SO, WHAT SHOULD WE DISCUSS?

Good news! Your discussions for National 5 can focus on almost anything inspired by literature, language or the media. That leaves the field fairly open.

We'll look in more detail at some approaches – but, at the moment let's see what literature, language and media sources might be used and how they might be handled.

Let's look first at poetry and suggest one way in which it might be used as a starting point for interactive discussion.

'Still I rise'
by Maya Angelou

You may write me down in history
With your bitter, twisted lies,
You may trod me in the very dirt
But still, like dust, I'll rise.

Does my sassiness upset you?
Why are you beset with gloom?
'Cause I walk like I've got oil wells
Pumping in my living room.

Just like moons and like suns,
With the certainty of tides,
Just like hopes springing high,
Still I'll rise.

Did you want to see me broken?
Bowed head and lowered eyes?
Shoulders falling down like teardrops.
Weakened by my soulful cries.

Does my haughtiness offend you?
Don't you take it awful hard
'Cause I laugh like I've got gold mines
Diggin' in my own back yard.

You may shoot me with your words,
You may cut me with your eyes,
You may kill me with your hatefulness,
But still, like air, I'll rise.

Does my sexiness upset you?
Does it come as a surprise
That I dance like I've got diamonds
At the meeting of my thighs?

Out of the huts of history's shame
I rise
Up from a past that's rooted in pain
I rise
I'm a black ocean, leaping and wide,
Welling and swelling I bear in the tide.
Leaving behind nights of terror and fear
I rise
Into a daybreak that's wondrously clear
I rise
Bringing the gifts that my ancestors gave,
I am the dream and the hope of the slave.
I rise
I rise
I rise.

POETRY-SOURCED MATERIAL

- Before forming your groups, read two poems on a related subject.
- Consider the audience(s) each may have appealed to.
- Indicate evidence for your answers.
- Examine in detail the techniques employed by each poet.
- What do they suggest about the poets' attitudes to their subjects?
- How effective do you consider each poem to be?
- Research any background information that you feel may deepen your understanding of the poems.

EXAMPLE:

'*Futility*' by Wilfred Owen and '*The Soldier*' by Rupert Brooke are both poems written about the First World War but from very different perspectives. Researching the background date and circumstances of each poem and poet will greatly enrich any later discussion.

HOW MIGHT THAT WORK IN PRACTICE?

The above example is an outline suggestion for approaching a discussion, but let's look in more detail at how we might go about preparing our discussion.

Here are two poems written at various points in the twentieth century. Start by reading them over.

'Strange Fruit'
by Abel Meeropol (pen-name Lewis Allan)

Southern trees bear a strange fruit,
Blood on the leaves and blood at the root,
Black bodies swinging in the southern breeze,
Strange fruit hanging from the poplar trees.

Pastoral scene of the gallant south,
The bulging eyes and the twisted mouth,
Scent of magnolias, sweet and fresh,
Then the sudden smell of burning flesh.

Here is fruit for the crows to pluck,
For the rain to gather, for the wind to suck,
For the sun to rot, for the trees to drop,
Here is a strange and bitter crop.

contd

There are a variety of pre-discussion tasks which might be carried out here, some by all members of the group, some by members self-selected or selected by your teacher.

- All participants should read both poems, making notes on the **imagery**, rhythm and use of contrast in each poem.

- Some members should investigate the known facts of Abel Meeropol and the background and date of the poem.

- Another task might be for other participants to investigate the legal position and social treatment of black people in America at the time of writing of the first poem.

- Others may wish to research briefly the biography of Maya Angelou and her position in literature.

- Some may wish to examine advances made in the position and role of black people in America in the years which intervene between the first and second poem and how these advances came about.

VIDEO LINK

Check this out! Before you start your discussion, try to watch and listen to Billie Holiday singing 'Strange Fruit' and then watch Maya Angelou introducing and then reciting 'And Still I Rise': www.brightredbooks.net/ N5English.

YOUR DISCUSSION

The final format for this might best be agreed by individual groups in consultation with their chairperson or teacher but might include:

- Introduction by chairperson

- Presentation of research findings

- Each member to suggest the audience most likely to read these poems? Consider: age and/or interests and/or nationality and/or another identified audience.

- Each member to explain with evidence from poems how this conclusion was reached.

- Personal response to each poem, with focus on the poetic techniques through which poets' attitudes are conveyed.

- In making its point(s), was one poem more successful in so doing? Give reasons for your answer.

- Summary of responses by reporter for the class in general.

DON'T FORGET

Remember that, for the purposes of your discussion, your notes should not be overly long. They need to be full but not so long that your presentation of them holds up the final discussion.

A satisfying outcome depends largely on the quality of the focus questions selected. These should be of the kind that allows scope for a variety of opinions and views.

In addition, before launching into the discussion, time should be allowed to the group members to reflect on what their own ideas are in relation to the focus questions. Not everyone is good at coming up with instant responses.

Remember, too, what was said earlier about the value of taking notes throughout the discussion. Discussions often move on quickly, so you don't want to forget the important point that occurred to you while another group member was talking.

ONLINE TEST

To test your knowledge of forming a group discussion around poetry, visit www. brightredbooks.net/ N5English.

THINGS TO DO AND THINK ABOUT

The poems 'In Mrs Tilscher's Class' by Carol Ann Duffy and 'Death of a Naturalist' by Seamus Heaney both explore, in very different settings, how children develop and learn from experience. You could very fruitfully examine how these two poets treat childhood and the end of innocence. Does either poem remind you of any episode in your earlier life? Consider and discuss your ideas on this topic with your group.

OTHER SOURCES OF INTERACTION

The approach outlined in the previous pages can work just as well should you choose to highlight some aspect of a novel, short story or play for discussion.

APPROACHING THE DISCUSSION

The approach to this discussion should include the following:

- Researching various aspects of the text's social background – for example, the reasons for the Stuarts' popularity/unpopularity before and after the Forty-Five Rebellion if you were reading, say, Robert Louis Stevenson's *Kidnapped*. Or the facts regarding the witch trials and the political climate of the USA after the Second World War if you were reading Arthur Miller's *The Crucible*.

- Note-taking/pre-discussion reflection on focus questions – for example, to what extent is a certain character responsible for his/her fate? For whom do you feel most sympathy? How did the writer help you to arrive at this response?

- Presenting research findings.

- Discussing focus questions.

- Summarising the responses by reporter.

- Possibly using the research for a later essay/report.

LANGUAGE-SOURCED INTERACTIONS

A news item or opinion piece might prove a useful source for discussion. A report or a comment piece where the group's sympathies might be divided would perhaps be most profitable. Your group could take turns to produce suitable material.

ELECTRONIC MEDIA-SOURCED INTERACTIONS

Here again, there is no shortage of material. A television programme or film with which everyone is familiar would work well. But be careful to focus attention on some particular questions; a generalised airing of opinions would perhaps not be too productive as an extended discussion.

- Background information on production history, casting difficulties, critical reception and popular reaction might all be useful areas to research.

- Think also about key scenes, use of music/sound effects and camera angles as the basis for focus questions.

- To what extent did these features help to determine your response?

What you have been studying here are, at one level, some useful guidelines for successful group interactions. But don't lose sight of the fact that getting involved in interactions of this kind also provides you profitably with tested material for discursive essays in either persuasive or argumentative form. Thanks to the varied inputs, there will be renewed depth and perspective to the topic, now that it has had the benefit of not only your own thoughts but also the thoughts of your group.

THINGS TO DO AND THINK ABOUT

Here are two pieces on a related subject. Read them over.

In praise of … texting

Formless and too often forgettable, the phone conversation has at last been replaced by pithy, editable, retrievable texts.

Let joy be unconfined. After a hundred years, the dominance of the ubiquitous instrument of intrusion that is the telephone has been challenged. Its day is over (or at least fading): the shrill, demanding call for attention, right now, has been toppled. Formless and too often forgettable, the phone conversation has at last been replaced by pithy, editable, retrievable texts. Texting (and being texted) has just the right amount of contact and non-contact. Emails are for business, and increasingly phone calls are for aged relatives. With its capacity to do everything in between, texting is now more popular than phoning among under-24s, Ofcom has found. Not surprisingly, for texts can be an urgent dialogue or a languorous conversation, a blushing apology or a declaration of undying love. If necessary, they can even set up a phone call. Above all, a texter can polish their message to an art form; and the recipient can choose when – or if – to respond.

(*Guardian* editorial, 18 July 2012)

Talk is cheap, but texting is cheaper

Simple arrangements such as meeting for a drink can take five exchanges.

Does it matter that my child is on the other side of the world and we haven't exchanged a word? Or rather, we haven't exchanged a spoken word. We have texted. And texting, as we know from a new Ofcom survey, has overtaken voice calling as our preferred method of communication. We now send on average 50 text messages a week, double the number we did in 2008. Last year, we spent 5 per cent less time on the phone than in 2010.

I'm part of the problem, not the solution. Some of the 150 billion messages sent last year were from me: a brief scroll through my BlackBerry reveals such classics as 'chicken or tuna?' and 'come home NOW'.

What that shows, of course, is that a text message is a terribly inefficient, inarticulate tool. I try always to be clear, but simple arrangements such as meeting up for a drink can take four or five exchanges; and that quip you might make to somebody about not splitting a bill equally can be read as a terse judgement without the crucial tone-of-voice 'banter' alert.

The kid texting 'I love it here, I'm considering staying' might well be joking about his Mexican holiday but how the hell do I know? I suspect fear is the driving force behind this text, as so many others. We have become fearful of voice communication, of revealing too much with our voices or being expected to concentrate, listen and respond in a meaningful way, like, on demand.

Who among us hasn't bailed out of an arrangement with a shady 'Sorry, stuck at the office'? How much kinder to speak your excuses: unless you have Facetime, a phone spares your blushes.

More troubling still is this: if 58 per cent of adults send messages each day to friends and family, how do the older generation fit in? I realise that my reliance on texting, my shaming shying-away from speech, means that I am rarely in touch with my parents. It's so much easier to text a 'how are you?' than risk getting caught for a 10-minute update on Aunt Virginia's health. My father never has his mobile switched on (he's so proud that the battery lasts six weeks at a time). Is it really never the right moment to ring any more?

We might feel a small sense of satisfaction that after years of stiffing us on mobile call charges, our switch to texting is denying the service providers some profit. I'm not sure that we're really texting it to The Man.

What we're gaining is the ability to fly our thumbs over the keys with increasing speed, and to negotiate pavements while gazing down at our mobiles. But what we're losing is something more profound: our voices.

(Lisa Markwell, *The Independent*, 19 July 2012)

Instructions:

- Select pair(s) from group to summarise the arguments of each writer.

- The group should then evaluate the accuracy of their reported findings.

- To whom would each article most likely appeal? Consider gender, age, interests when answering.

- Give reasons for your answers.

- Which view of the two writers do you find the more convincing?

- Which arguments put forward swayed your opinion?

- How would you describe the tone of each writer addressing the issue? Point to evidence to justify your answer.

LOST FOR WORDS?

Follow the suggestions in this chapter and you are well on your way to making a success of your group discussions for National 5. The topic you choose will often determine the final format of the interaction: sometimes you will reach an agreement (or **consensus**), at other times you won't. The point is to bring an open mind, informed opinion, clear expression and tolerance of others to your deliberations.

Remember, too, that the hard work and the focus you have brought to many of these discussions are bringing you rewards well beyond successful completion of your National 5 course. The ability to interact effectively in a group is a key to success in university and college seminars and tutorials; it will also be an important element in functioning well in whatever career you take up in later life.

ONLINE

You can find suggested possible solutions in the 'Answers' section in our Digital Zone: www.brightredbooks.net/N5English

TASK

This group is in trouble! The discussion on solar energy is not going well. The group members all have different problems. They need help to formulate the kind of language that will get the discussion moving on over this bad patch.

Challenge 1

Suggest <u>three</u> different statements phrased in the kind of language you think appropriate for each situation. Remember, your wording may vary but it needs to catch the <u>tone</u> of the suggested solution.

Challenge 2

Share and discuss with each other the suitability of the wording of your solutions before going online for the suggestions made there. Were you in rough agreement?

ONLINE TEST ✔

To test your overall knowledge of group discussions, take the 'Lost for words' test at www.brightredbooks.net/N5English.

'I really don't have anything to say here. But I need to say something!'

'If they go on about this point much longer, I'll nod off.'

Craig

Francesca

THINGS TO DO AND THINK ABOUT

Now it's your turn.

Stage your own group discussion on solar energy.

How well did you do? Be honest! Use the grid below to check out what you think your group's performance was. Where you were weak, how would you go about remedying the problem?

Now, there's *another* discussion for you!

DON'T FORGET

At all costs, the discussion needs to be kept moving on. Drifting off mentally, failing to engage with key points or showing impatience or boredom with others are all barriers to a full exploration of any topic.

	Weak	Satisfactory	Really successful
Balance of contributions			
Interaction of contributors			
Content of points made			
Overall tone of discussion			
Body language			
Chairperson's management			
Summary quality			

'They've completely misunderstood. I need to put a stop to this. Mark is right.'

'I'm lost, but I don't want to look a numptie!'

'If I don't stop Mark soon, there's going to be a stand-up fight here.'

'These people have no idea what they're talking about!'

Sean

Gail

Chairperson Claire

Mark

THE IMPORTANCE OF EFFECTIVE LISTENING

Earlier in our group-discussion section, we stressed the importance of being an active listener in the context of group work: the need to interpret not only the oral message but also the equally important non-verbal one, signalled by body language, facial expression, tone and gestures. The aim of the speaker and purposes of the contribution are also key considerations here. All play their part in listening productively to a speaker.

TIME SPENT COMMUNICATING

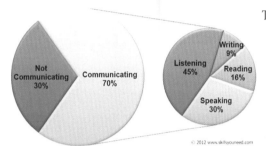

Based on the research of R. Adler, L. Rosenfeld and R. Proctor (2001), *Interplay: The Process of Interpersonal Communicating*, Fort Worth, TX: Harcourt

The usefulness of being fully attuned to verbally communicated information, however, extends far beyond its importance in group discussions. If you look for a minute at these pie-charts, you will see just how important listening is.

These research findings highlight the amazing amount of time we spend each day in overall communicating activities. In this Study Guide, a great deal of time is being devoted to improving your effectiveness in terms of reading, writing and speaking. Rightly so, since together they occupy 55% of our communicating efforts. But let's think for a minute about that other 45%, the time spent listening.

ONLINE

Check out the article, 'Shut Up: How Great Leaders Listen' about how important listening skills are in business: www.brightredbooks.net/N5English.

ONLINE TEST

Test yourself on listening skills online at www.brightredbooks.net/N5English.

LEARNING TO BE AN EFFECTIVE LISTENER

How much of our education has been spent on teaching us how to be effective listeners? Probably very little so far, since there seems to be a fairly general misconception that listening is the same as hearing – and nobody teaches us how to hear now, do they?

But, given the substantial proportion of our communicating time spent on listening, perhaps the moment has come to give it more attention and to study it just as actively as the other three skills.

Think for a minute, too, how much of your learning to date has been acquired through listening to teachers, broadcasters, instructors and fellow students. Developed more intensively, this key learning channel will be fundamental to advancing your studies still further. So, let's see how that can be done.

THE BARRIERS TO ACTIVE LISTENING

If we're honest with ourselves, we all have a tendency to be passive listeners. We switch on the TV, we select an MP3 track, we ask a friend how they are – and then we get distracted. The sounds carry on, but our mind is often elsewhere, although, if challenged, we will hotly claim that we have been 'listening'.

Wandering attention is the enemy of active listening. Active listening requires sustained effort, an effort that we do not always make. Distractions are everywhere, and our attention span is easily disturbed. If you're doubtful about the accuracy of that, try this next activity.

THINGS TO DO AND THINK ABOUT

The simple online audio exercise in listening for specifics on page 22 may well demonstrate the fact that our concentration cannot always be fully trusted, even when all we have to focus on is the information itself. In a real-life situation, that concentration can be further distracted by local conditions: what we feel about the person we're listening to, the noise in the room, the view outside, to name just a few. So, let's sample listening in a real-life situation to see how you get on.

Organise yourselves into groups of three. In the group, one member will talk, one will listen and a third will take notes of what is said by the talker. You can take turns at being talker/listener/reporter. Give yourself about 15 minutes for each of you to organise your thoughts around one of the following topics. Start only when everyone has had time to decide what they are going to say. The more detail, the better.

Once the talker and note-taker are ready to start, the listener will behave as follows:

WILL ✓	WILL NOT ✗
Listen without reacting obviously to what is said	Interrupt
Face the talker in a relaxed position	Fidget
Maintain eye contact	Tune out from spoken content

Talker should speak informally and naturally on the following topics in sequence without allowing for any lengthy pause between topics:

1 *'Once I complete my education, I would like to ...'* complete with a minimum 4–5 sentences considering various possibilities: for example, travel the world (Why? Anywhere in particular? What do you think this would bring you?); move to another part of the country (Why? Are you getting away from something? Or looking for something you don't have now?); get yourself a secure job; settle down and start a family. Be prepared to explain the reasons behind your choices.

2 *'If I were Prime Minister for a day, I would ...'* complete with a minimum 4–5 sentences considering various possibilities: for example, make changes to schools (What precisely? And why?); make changes to our health system (In what way? For what reasons?); ban smoking/raise price of alcohol. Be prepared to go into detail about any of these – or any other – possibilities.

3 *'Someone I really admire is ...'* complete with a minimum 4–5 sentences considering various possibilities: for example, someone in the history of your country; someone who has given the world a great invention; a famous painter/musician/sportsman; a member of your family/a friend. Be sure to give plenty of detail about why this person has gained your admiration.

The listener needs now to report back as fully as he/she can on what has just been said, while the talker and note-taker check for accuracy of the listener's response.

CHECK OUT	RESPONSE
How much of the original was retained?	
Was anything added/made up?	
Were there areas where the speaker seemed more involved than in others?	
What were these areas, and how was this signalled by the speaker?	

To optimise your future listening practices, we need to look carefully at how active listening can be improved. We need to eliminate any barriers in order to add real focus to your listening behaviour.

ONLINE

Before we embark on real-life listening situations, try the online listening game, 'BBC Skillswise: Listening for specifics' to check just how active your listening skills are when listening for simple specifics (www.brightredbooks.net/N5English). Scroll down to 'The Virtual Traveller Game'. Click on the New York trip, select the 'short' version and listen to it carefully, making notes as you listen. Once you have completed your notes, only then turn to the questions on page 22.

THE GOOD LISTENER'S CHARTER

So, what have our listening activities taught us so far? Probably that good listening is not as easy as it might first sound. As we go on to look at more complicated listening activities, you will notice that concentration on specific items of information is by no means the sole requirement or aim. Our work on group discussions has already taught you that listening is only part of a much more complex communication process. In short, we need more than a good pair of ears to listen effectively!

Attention to the aims of the speaker and the purpose of the communication; an alertness to differentiate the essential from the merely interesting; a sensitivity to the non-verbal: these are just some of the attributes of the active listener. Let's look in detail at how to listen more effectively.

EFFECTIVE LISTENING

Examine aims and purposes

What seem to you to be the speaker's aims here? Is it to convey information, to persuade you to adopt a certain viewpoint, to analyse a critical situation or simply to entertain? Perhaps the speaker will have more than one aim in the same communication and will, say, entertain us in order to persuade us to share a viewpoint. Be alert to such possible cross-overs. Monitor content constantly to ascertain central aims. Check, too, whether the ideas are being backed by convincing information/statistics or are merely claims or opinions.

Adopt a positive attitude to the subject

Perhaps, on the surface, the subject does not appear particularly interesting to you. You cannot, however, afford to lose concentration. The greatest mark-loser is to listen passively, letting the information wash over you. Listen actively; do not make negative assumptions about the interest or complexity of what you are going to hear; stay alert. You may be surprised by the turn the talk takes.

Adopt a positive attitude to the speaker

Ignore distractions such as appearance, personality, weak delivery, accent or mannerisms. It's the message, not the messenger, that counts. And do not lose concentration or patience because they adopt an opinion that does not coincide with yours.

Avoid external distractions

The view from the window, whispering behind you, the heat in the room, pre-lunch rumbling from your stomach – these are all very human distractions which can disturb concentration long enough to miss a key point.

contd

Concentrate on central ideas

Don't let interesting stories or examples blind you to the reason for their inclusion in the talk. They are there to illustrate a point; they are not usually the point in themselves. Are there clues in the opening statements that indicate what the central ideas of the upcoming sections might be? Note them down. Listen for ideas, not individual words.

Be alert to the non-verbal

The emotional tone of the speaker may be saying as much, or more, about underlying feelings as the surface content of his or her words. Emotions are less easy to control than words. Skilled listening means listening for messages which the speaker's voice, rather than words, may be unconsciously signalling. As in group discussion, body language can also give hints to the real message.

Make notes that matter

Trying to jot down everything that's said is not only impossible, it's distracting you from what *is* being said. Make notes brief, concentrating on key ideas and key words or phrases. And write them so that they are readable afterwards!

UNDERSTANDING SPEAKERS AND THEIR AIMS

Making sense of spoken communication, as we are seeing, requires us to be alert on several fronts. As well as being tuned in to the factual information being presented, we need also to listen for signals which tell us the intended **purpose** of the communication and the **audience** at whom it is aimed. Alert to these considerations, we are better equipped to understand and assess the speaker's success or failure in communicating with us.

Identifying purpose

Whether in a group discussion, a lecture or a talk, a speaker's purposes may be many and various. Let's take a look at four of the more common aims and the kind of language that might be used to realise these aims.

Purpose	Some possible markers
Inform	Neutral, unemotional language Balanced arguments and structure Factual reporting
Analyse	Subject-specific vocabulary Technical statistics and data Complex sentences
Persuade	Emotive vocabulary **Rhetorical questions** **Repetition** Targeted climaxes
Entertain	Colloquial vocabulary Chatty expressions, short sentences **Anecdotes** Exaggeration

VIDEO LINK

Check out this clip about active listening: 'How to be a good listener: Good listeners: Active listening' at www.brightredbooks.net/N5English.

DON'T FORGET

In the course of the address, the speaker may have more than one purpose. If, for example, the intention is **to persuade** or **to inform** us, then he/she may want **to entertain** us in places in order to make the point all the more effective. Be alert to shifts of approach and what lies behind them.

ONLINE TEST

Test yourself on the good listener's charter online at www.brightredbooks.net/N5English.

THINGS TO DO AND THINK ABOUT

Type 'Cameron Russell: Looks aren't everything. Believe me, I'm a model' (www.ted.com) into your browser and then watch and listen to the TED talk. Make notes as you listen.

Now, once you have listened and watched, you may wish to check your receptivity to what you have heard in various ways. Here are two possibilities:

- Listen and watch a first time to find out how focused your concentration has been on factual specifics. Then try Focus Questions on page 22.

- Listen and watch a second time, not only to determine factual detail but also to evaluate the effectiveness of the speaker and her aims and purposes in addressing her audience. And which specific audience does she have in mind here? Then try Generic Questions on page 23.

UNIT ACTIVITIES

Now that you have learned about how to listen effectively, try out these activity worksheets. Follow the instructions from the 'Online' activity on page 19 and the 'Things to Do and Think about' activity on page 21 before attempting these questions.

NEW YORK QUESTION SHEET

1 In what way did the tourist find walking down Fifth Avenue dangerous?   2

2 He refused to break-dance for what reason?   1

3 The Empire State Building has its Observatory on (a) the top floor, (b) the 86th floor, (c) the 102nd floor?   2

4 Name three states that can be seen from the Observatory.   3

5 Name four attractions to be enjoyed in Central Park.   4

6 Broadway is to be found between which two streets?   2

7 What did the tourist find difficult to believe about Broadway?   1

8 Why did he not go to the theatre? (a) He needed a cup of coffee, (b) he ran out of time, (c) he visited the Statue of Liberty instead?   2

Being more thoughtful:

9 Reflecting on the talk as a whole, what can we infer about the visitor's reaction to New York? What evidence would you point to in order to support your answer?   2

10 Referring back to the Purpose grid on page 21, what do you believe to be the speaker's intentions in giving this talk? What evidence can you give for your answer?   2

21 marks total

DON'T FORGET ✚

If you only listened to Cameron Russell's talk once, answer the focus questions. If you have listened to the talk twice, answer the generic questions.

'LOOKS AREN'T EVERYTHING. BELIEVE ME, I'M A MODEL'

FOCUS QUESTIONS

1 Identify what you consider to be the principal purpose – or purposes – of this talk. Give reasons for your answer, referring to the grid on page 21 for assistance if necessary.   4

2 Cameron Russell says she has two reasons for that change of appearance she makes on stage. What are the reasons?   2

3 A few minutes into the talk, Russell indicates the formal structure she is going to impose on her talk. What is this structure, and does she adhere to it?   2

4 Russell gives two reasons to explain why she succeeded in becoming a model: 'I won a genetic lottery and I am the recipient of a legacy'. In your own words as far as possible, explain what she means by this.   4

5 Why does Russell think it is foolish for young girls to say they want to be a model when they grow up?   2

6 '10 years of accumulated model knowledge can be distilled ... into right now.' Russell then proceeds to demonstrate this 'accumulated knowledge'. What is she implying about this knowledge by the demonstration she gives?   2

contd

7 At one point, Russell shows a series of pictures where her model self is pictured on the left and her real self is pictured on the right. She says the pictures on the left are not of her but of 'constructions'. In your own words, explain what she means by this. 3

8 She seems rather unhappy about 'the free stuff she gets in real life'. In your own words, explain the reasons why being judged by her appearance is disturbing for her.
2

9 Russell is honest in her appraisal of a model's life, appreciating the privileges she enjoys but being aware of a downside to this career. What is that downside? 2

10 Judging by all aspects of the talk you have listened to, suggest the audience for which it is intended, giving evidence for your answer. 2

25 marks total

GENERIC QUESTIONS

1 (a) Although given here before a fairly general audience, for whom, in your opinion, would this talk be of most interest? You may consider:

- age
- interests
- gender
- nationality
- class 2

(b) What evidence helped you reach this conclusion? 4

2 Sum up Russell's overall view of modelling as a career. What evidence would you indicate to back up your assessment? 6

3 How convincing did Russell seem to you to be as a speaker? You could consider:

- her attitude to her career
- her choice of clothing
- her gestures/mannerisms
- her tone of voice
- her attitude to others 4

4 With the help of the above grid, suggest what you think the purpose – or purposes – of this talk might be. 2

5 Explain your reasons for thinking this. 2

20 marks total

ONLINE

To get the answers to these questions, visit www.brightredbooks.net/N5English

ONLINE TEST

For more questions on these listening exercises, visit www.brightredbooks.net/N5English

THINGS TO DO AND THINK ABOUT

Have a look at the next page to see how well these activities have covered the unit outcomes of your National 5 English course!

OUTCOMES CHECK

Now, you and your teacher may simply want to make use of the activities we've been suggesting as helpful practice sessions before assessing Unit Outcomes. But look closely at them again and you'll see that, if skilfully managed, they can generate evidence which will cover a variety of Unit Outcome requirements.

CREATION AND PRODUCTION UNIT: OUTCOME 2

First of all, the group discussions you have become involved in fulfil Outcome 2 of your Creation and Production Unit. How so? Well, if you have researched and structured your contribution to the various interactions as fully as we have suggested here, and if you have taken part in them appropriately, using body language/eye contact to good effect, you are demonstrating your ability to take part in detailed spoken interactions by:

2.1 Selecting significant ideas and content, using a format and structure appropriate to purposes and audience

2.2 Applying knowledge and understanding of language in terms of language choice

2.3 Communicating meaning at a first hearing

2.4 Using significant aspects of non-verbal communication

ANALYSIS AND EVALUATION UNIT: OUTCOME 2

By listening carefully to the Cameron Russell talk in our Listening Comprehension section and answering the generic questions we suggested on page 23, you are fulfilling the requirements of Outcome 2 of Analysis and Evaluation Unit in that you can demonstrate an ability to understand, analyse and evaluate detailed spoken language by:

2.1 Identifying and explaining the purpose and audience

2.2 Identifying and explaining the main ideas and supporting details

2.3 Applying knowledge and understanding of language to explain meaning and effect

CREATION AND PRODUCTION UNIT: OUTCOME 1

You are also in a position to fulfil the requirements of Outcome 1 of the Creation and Production Unit through transforming some of the research work you have been doing to prepare for the Spoken Interactions into essay form. (If, alternatively, you are keen to pursue other ideas – in persuasive or discursive mode – which you are researching for the Folio, these can be written about, too, to fulfil these requirements.) This Outcome requires you to create and produce detailed written texts by:

1.1 Selecting significant ideas and content, using a format and structure appropriate to the purpose and audience

1.2 Applying knowledge and understanding of language in terms of language choice and technical accuracy

1.3 Communicating meaning at first reading

Any help you need for using appropriate format and structure referred to above is well provided in the Folio section of this Study Guide. Check it out.

ANALYSIS AND EVALUATION UNIT: OUTCOME 1

And so, finally, how can you fulfil the requirements of Outcome 1 of the Analysis and Evaluation Unit? Again, your work in Spoken Interactions has helped you well on your way to demonstrating that you can understand, analyse and evaluate detailed written texts by:

1.1 Identifying and explaining the purposes and audience, as appropriate to genre

1.2 Identifying and explaining the main ideas and supporting details

1.3 Applying knowledge and understanding of language to explain meaning and effect, using appropriate critical terminology

If you used the poems and newspaper articles earlier in this section as the source material for group discussion and followed our detailed suggestions for analysis of each genre, you are well placed to fulfil these requirements. Your teacher may have made a detailed checklist of your responses, or may have made full observation notes as you discussed them, or may have set you detailed written questions on the aims, purposes and techniques of the writers to make their chosen effects. Whatever the final chosen method, however, your Unit experiences here will usefully complement your understanding, analysis and evaluation skills not only in Close Reading but also in your Critical Reading of the Scottish texts in the final exam.

 ## THINGS TO DO AND THINK ABOUT

As we said right at the beginning of this section, the required Outcomes of the National 5 Units can be fulfilled in a variety of very satisfying ways for learner and teacher alike. But still more important than fulfilling course requirements satisfactorily, however, is the fact that these activities will bring you rewards well beyond the course itself. For the ability to research, investigate, analyse, evaluate and thereafter interact effectively and productively in a group is key to success in university and college seminars and tutorials. It will also provide a vital element in helping you function well in whatever career you take up in later life.

READING FOR UNDERSTANDING, ANALYSIS AND EVALUATION: WAYS OF SUCCEEDING

AN OVERVIEW

This paper (commonly referred to as the Close Reading paper) will represent 30 of the 70 marks of your final National 5 examination paper. As it forms such a significant proportion of your final grade, its challenges need to be fully met.

But what exactly will these challenges be? What kind of text, you may be asking yourself, will I be faced with? What type of questions will I be expected to answer? What kind of reading skills is it setting out to test? What question-answering techniques will I be expected to know? How do I set about learning them?

These are just a few of the questions to which we will be helping you find answers in this section of this book. So, let's get started.

THE TEXT

The text on which you will be asked to answer a series of questions will be selected by the examiners from a non-fiction text of distinction. Quality journalism, biography and travel writing are the kinds of texts you can expect to encounter. So, it would be wise to make sure you are familiar with writing of these genres long before the exam. Whatever form the final choice takes, the text in question will run to around 1000 words and will foreground the types of writing skills and techniques on which you will be expected to comment fully.

ONLINE

To test your knowledge of Close Reading questions and suitable answers, take the quiz at www.brightredbooks. net/N5English.

DON'T FORGET

Horses for courses. If a question is only worth 2 marks, don't waste 10 lines answering it; conversely, if it's worth 4 marks, a single line simply will not do.

THE QUESTIONS

You will be expected to answer questions which will test your ability to **understand**, **analyse** and **evaluate** the article's content in some detail. You will also be asked to give broader answers which will test your ability to **infer** the author's general intentions in certain areas of the text and to **summarise some key ideas**. The number of marks allocated to each question will be clearly marked, thus helping you to manage your time appropriately. Let's take a brief overview of what your responses need to cover in each of these categories.

contd

Understanding questions

These are by far the most straightforward questions to answer. They mean just what they say: they test your grasp of <u>what</u> the piece is all about and probe your understanding of certain items of vocabulary; you may also be asked to suggest <u>why</u> certain comments are made. Being able to paraphrase ideas and expressions from the text is of prime importance here.

Analysis questions

These are a bit more demanding. Here you need to look at <u>how</u> a writer created a certain effect, by identifying how certain techniques and words or phrases are used to create that effect. Here you will need to quote certain items from the text, identify the technique at work and suggest what its effect on the reader is.

Evaluation questions

These ask you for your opinion of <u>how well</u> you think something has been said. To do this, you will need to find items of evidence to back up your assessment: a particularly successful simile, for instance, or a striking contrast in the choice of words which will form the basis of your comment. You may well have commented on these already in an Analysis question, but now you need to develop your own 'take' on them.

Inference questions

These have elements in common with understanding questions. You need to understand what is being said not just directly, but indirectly too. You could call this 'reading between the lines'. Your ability to work this out and express your deductions in your own words tells the examiner that you are alert at reading subtle signals from the writer and are capable of responding accordingly.

Summarising questions

These demand an ability to take an indicated stretch of text and to extract from it only the key points. These you will need to express in your own words. Again, your understanding is being tested – but, given the higher marks usually involved, your answer may need to be more extended than other understanding questions.

THINGS TO DO AND THINK ABOUT

You will have read enough by now to know that the key to a successful Close Reading score is to *read quality non-fiction on a regular basis.* It might be a newspaper, it might be a biography, it might be travel writing, but make a point of making contact regularly with this kind of writing from today. Don't leave it until nearer the exam. The wider your reading, and the more extensive your vocabulary, the greater your chances of success.

THE READING-SKILLS FAMILY: THE UNDERSTANDING QUESTION

So, let's take a closer look at what these various types of question involve, and let's examine in detail how to go about answering them successfully.

THE UNDERSTANDING QUESTION: THE RANGE

These are by far the most straightforward questions you will encounter. They are there to test exactly what their name implies: your understanding of what you have been reading. These questions will often begin as follows:

Explain in your own words ...

*What is the meaning of ...? How does the **context** help you work it out?*

Why did the writer's mother ...?

In your opinion, who is ...? Give a reason for your answer.

What does the expression '...' tell you about the writer's frame of mind?

When you see questions which may begin this way, be aware that the examiners are testing not only your understanding of specific words or expressions but also your ability to express them in your own words. You cannot 'lift' sections of the sentence to provide an answer, because then you are avoiding the very test that is being set.

Using your own words

Be warned here! When explaining an idea 'in your own words' or giving an answer which is 'in your own opinion', don't automatically try a word-for-word 'translation'; you will often find this difficult. Try to explain the idea rather than find substitutes for individual words. For instance, suppose the answer to a question lay in the sentence:

Total-immersion courses based in Italian families are seen by some as a valid alternative to college studies.

Phrases such as 'total immersion' and 'valid alternative' could be tricky on a word-for-word basis, so avoid this by trying to reshape the sentence entirely as if you were explaining this to someone who was not sure what these phrases meant. Starting with somewhere else rather than 'Total immersion' might be a good idea. Perhaps start with 'Some people ...' or 'There are those who think ...'. This gives you:

Some people believe that living full-time with an Italian family is just as successful as studying Italian at college.

Or:

There are those who think that sharing life with an Italian family will benefit you as much learning Italian in a more academic setting.

DON'T FORGET

Unpack the *idea*, rather than substitute *one word for another*, when explaining in your own words or giving your own opinion in understanding questions.

What do I change?

Another word of caution: there are some words which you will not be expected to change. Here you will have to use your common sense. Proper nouns and common nouns with no obvious alternatives (e.g. 'crocodile', 'brakes', 'mortgage') need to stay as they are, but verbs, adverbs, adjectives and figures of speech will need to be rephrased.

Tracking down the answer

In Understanding questions, a good tip is to adopt a two-stage approach:

Stage 1: Highlight or underline the words or phrases in the text where you know the answers lie.

Stage 2: Work now on putting these words or phrases in a new way, perhaps reshaping the section entirely to make it your own.

THINGS TO DO AND THINK ABOUT

Let's try that out:

> Since the day the Romans stepped beyond Hadrian's Wall, enemy armies have probably come to a halt at the sight of the Scottish infantry: short, red-headed blokes who might at first look like stunted carrots, but turn out to be ferociously terrier-like. Their latter-day equivalents were the likes of Jimmy Johnstone and Billy Bremner, dinky-sized footballers who ran rings around their opponents, and in so doing gave their fellow gingers a much-needed confidence boost.

'Red hair is a beacon in a sea of mediocrity', Rosemary Goring, *Herald*, Monday 2 July 2012

Using your own words, explain why over the centuries it has been a mistake to judge Scottish soldiers and footballers by their appearance. 2

So, what are we to highlight? 'Over the centuries' suggests that we are looking for one reason from the distant past and maybe also a later one. (There are also two marks at stake, so two examples might be a good idea.) So, what surprised the Roman soldiers? Maybe the fact that these short men, who looked like 'stunted carrots', turned out 'to be ferociously terrier-like'? And, more recently, there were 'dinky-sized' footballers 'who ran rings round their opponents'? So, we are looking for our own way of constructing an answer from these highlighted items which together say *outwardly unusual (short, red-haired) – yet surprisingly effective, not just then but later, too.* So, how about this?

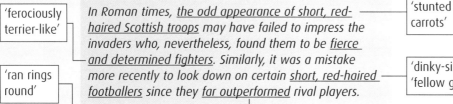

'ferociously terrier-like'

'ran rings round'

In Roman times, the odd appearance of short, red-haired Scottish troops may have failed to impress the invaders who, nevertheless, found them to be fierce and determined fighters. Similarly, it was a mistake more recently to look down on certain short, red-haired footballers since they far outperformed rival players.

'stunted carrots'

'dinky-sized' 'fellow gingers'

What about these answers?

With a partner – or as a class – look at these answers and say what kind of mark you would give them. Explain in detail your reasons for awarding your mark.

Although their appearance was against them, Scottish soldiers in Roman times were good fighters. More recently there have been good, short footballers.

Short, red-haired Scotsmen have always been good in battle and in sport.

In Roman times red-haired Scottish soldiers frightened the invaders and so have some red-haired footballers more recently.

Despite looking unusual, being short and red-haired, the Scottish soldiers never gave up on their fierce attacks on the Roman invaders. In later years, some Scottish footballers of similar appearance were equally effective when confronting the opposition.

Things to remember:

- Being able to explain ideas and concepts in your own words lies at the heart of successfully answering understanding questions.

- Get into the way of selecting random sentences from quality journalism and turning their ideas into your own language.

- Avoid 'translations'; don't become a prisoner of the writer's word order; turn the sentence around to suit your own style of talking or writing.

- Highlight all the relevant points, making sure you cover *all* the highlighted points when you come to phrase your own answer.

DON'T FORGET

Proper nouns/common nouns with no obvious alternatives

No change! ✗

Common nouns with clear alternatives, verbs, adverbs, adjectives, figures of speech

All change! ✓

UNDERSTANDING QUESTIONS: PRACTICE

Here are some more questions on extracts from Rosemary Goring's article 'Red hair is a beacon in a sea of mediocrity', featured in the *Herald*, Monday 2 July 2012:

1   When you think of how many talented redheads we've had, from Mary, Queen of Scots to Ewan McGregor, it's anyone's guess where the stigma comes from. Some, apparently, used to think it was a sign of immorality, as if devilish flames were licking around the person's head. Personally, I love it: whether it's a Tilda Swinton burnt orange, or a Robert Redford strawberry blonde, all reds are beautiful. Sadly, though, not everyone would agree. And perhaps because women have been more easily able to disguise their natural shade, it's men who continue to bear the brunt of an entrenched prejudice which, under the term 'gingerism', is deemed by some to be as serious a form of discrimination as racism.

(a) Using your own words, give two reasons why the writer believes criticism of redheads is unjustified.   2

(b) What is the meaning of 'stigma'? How did the context help you work this out?   2

(c) What does the expression 'entrenched prejudice' suggest about the public's view of male redheads?   2

(d) Explain in your own words what the writer means by 'gingerism'.   2

2   So, even though chemists' shelves abound in russet hair-dyes, the fear of red lives on. Admittedly there was a flurry of interest in redheaded men when the American thriller *Homeland* was aired this spring with Damien Lewis in the main role. A glance at Lewis's career, however, shows that he's made a living playing sinister characters, as if his coppery thatch was a convenient shorthand for viewers. Benedict Cumberbatch, meanwhile, toned himself down to a dull brown to play Sherlock Holmes, and Michael C. Hall, from *Dexter* and *Six Feet Under*, is boringly mousy in both series when in reality he could effortlessly hide himself in a field of pumpkins.

(a) Using your own words, explain why the writer believes 'the fear of red lives on'.   2

(b) Explain in your own words why a 'coppery thatch was a convenient shorthand for viewers' in the selection of Damien Lewis for this particular role.   2

3   I simply don't understand why anyone would camouflage themselves as brunette or black or even blonde when they could stand out like a lighted match, a flaring beacon in a sea of mediocrity. I just hope Merida's crimson curls mean redheads finally get the respect they deserve. Otherwise, they will surely soon be dyed out of existence.

(a) What does the expression 'a flaring beacon in a sea of mediocrity' suggest about the writer's view of red-haired people?   2

(b) In your own words, suggest what the writer means by claiming that redheads will 'soon be dyed out of existence'   1

Check your answer with a partner's, and get a third person to comment on how fully each of you has fulfilled the demands of the question, avoiding as far as possible any use of words from the original text. Only then look up the suggestions for answers on our Digital Zone.

ONLINE TEST

For more practice at understanding questions, test yourself online at www. brightredbooks.net/N5English

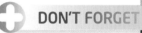

DON'T FORGET

There is more than one way of expressing an answer to any of these questions.

DON'T FORGET

Understanding questions do not just test your comprehension of information; they also put your vocabulary under the spotlight. You must not fudge this with 'lifts' from the writer's text. Are you working on developing vocabulary by regular reading of quality journalism? If not, it's time you started!

THINGS TO DO AND THINK ABOUT

Comment with a partner on the following answers to question 1 (a) above. You need to consider not just the accuracy or otherwise of the comment, but also to what extent the students have used their own words. How many marks out of two would you award each one?

I. Since we've had many talented redheads from Mary Queen of Scots to Ewan McGregor, it's anyone's guess why they are disliked. She also thinks they are all beautiful.

II. She believes that over the centuries there have been many able, clever redheads, which make this criticism unjustified. She also feels that people with red hair are most attractive.

III. She does not know where the stigma comes from, and in her opinion it is not a sign of immorality as was once thought.

IV. Mary Queen of Scots and Ewan McGregor show that having red hair shows talent, and in addition she finds them to be very attractive.

THE READING-SKILLS FAMILY: THE ANALYSIS QUESTION

ANALYSIS QUESTION: THE RANGE

Analysis questions are sometimes thought to be a little trickier to answer than understanding ones. They are there to test your ability to analyse *how* writers make their effects on readers. These questions demand a little more from you and may carry more than two marks to reflect this.

Normally you will need to do three things:

1 <u>Locate</u> relevant words or phrases from the text for your answer – again, highlighting these is a good idea.

2 <u>Identify</u> aspects of style at work: for example, simile, inverted sentence structure, list and so on.

3 <u>Explain</u> in your own words the <u>effect</u> this item is having on readers.

The Analysis questions can often be identified by their frequent use of the word <u>how</u>:

Comment on how the writer's use of imagery shows ...

How does the writer convey his fear of ...?

Suggest how the writer shows her disapproval of ...

But, be careful! The Analysis question may be expressed in other ways also:

Explain fully the appropriateness of the word ...

Quote an expression from the first sentence which ...

Comment on the effectiveness of the sentence structure ...

Identify and briefly explain the writer's use of ...

These are just some of the ways you will be expected to show your analytical skills in exploring the text in question.

LITERAL LANGUAGE VERSUS FIGURATIVE LANGUAGE

Before we go any further in tackling analysis questions, it will help if we sort out the distinction between **literal** language and **figurative language**.

In understanding questions, we are often being asked about the literal meaning of statements made or information given in the text:

> *What reasons does the writer give for ...?*
>
> *Explain why the writer dislikes ...*
>
> *Explain what the writer means by 'silent witness' in the first sentence.*

In other words, the questions are testing our powers of understanding words in their everyday or dictionary meaning. If, for instance, we say:

> *Our fields were in great need of water, and many communities went hungry*

we are talking in literal language. But if we say:

> *Our fields were crying out for water, and famine stalked the land*

we have changed from literal to figurative language.

Put simply, figurative language puts 'figures' (or pictures or images) into our text which help to convey the meaning much more vividly and dramatically than literal language. Not only has information about

contd

DON'T FORGET ✚

If you find yourself answering an analysis question without short quotations from the text, there is usually something far wrong! Questions asking you to comment on sentence structure might be an exception, but even here sufficient quotation should be given to identify which sentence or part of the sentence is being discussed.

shortage of water and risk of starvation been conveyed, but also it has been conveyed in a way which created illustrations in our imaginations. For here the fields are presented almost as people, shouting out to demand water, while famine, like some evil threatening giant, prowls around the communities.

Figurative language not only conveys meaning; it also pictures meaning. And, as the saying goes, a picture is worth a thousand words.

FIGURATIVE-LANGUAGE TECHNIQUES

Some analysis questions may test your knowledge of the various techniques that writers employ to create the images in figurative language. You are expected to comment on these. So, you need to locate what you see as an appropriate illustration of this technique: '*the buzzing of bees*', '*like a thief in the night*', identify it: *alliteration, simile*, and then explain what effect this choice by the writer is having on the reader. Before going further, you need to be sure of what figurative-language techniques are available to authors. Let's look at them.

DON'T FORGET

Your knowledge of figurative language needs to be really thorough – not just for your **Close Reading** work but also for writing **Critical Essays** and **Context** work.

The English language is rich in figurative-language devices, and a full list of some of the most common can be found in the Glossary at the end of this book. There are some, however, which tend to be found frequently in exams of this kind.

These devices fall broadly into two categories: those which conjure up visual pictures, and those which create pictures in sound – aural pictures, you might say.

VISUAL IMAGERY	AURAL IMAGERY
Simile: a comparison between two items using 'like' or 'as'. *He's like a dog with a bone.* The effect of similes and metaphors is to add pictorial emphasis/impact to the written description.	**Alliteration**: the repetition of a particular consonant – or consonant sound – at the beginning of a group of words to create a certain sound effect. *Cold clay clads his coffin.* Here the harsh sound of the letter 'c' matches the grimness of the description. *Soft sighing of the southern seas.* Here the soft 's' sounds mimics the gentleness of the water's sound.
Metaphor: also a comparison, but this time the two items being compared are not 'like' each other, since one item becomes the other. *You're an angel.*	**Assonance**: the repetition of a certain group of similar-sounding vowels in words close to each other, again used to create a certain aural effect. *And murmuring of innumerable bees.*
Personification: yet another way of making a comparison. Similes and metaphors can become examples of personification when an inanimate object (without life) is spoken of as if it were human and alive. *The wind howled down the corridor.*	**Onomatopoeia**: here the sound of the word mimics its meaning. *Clink, fizz, rip, honk, boom, purr* suggest their meaning in their sound.
Hyperbole: an exaggerated image to create a certain effect (often humorous) or to emphasise something. *The list goes on for miles. He never fails to get lost.*	**Enjambment**: in poetry, this is the running-on of one line into another or into several others, often to give either a conversational feel to the content or sometimes to suggest a speeding-up for an effect of urgency. It can also make the reader wait for a key point to be made when the sentence finally stops. *... for my purpose holds To sail beyond the sunset, and the baths Of all the western stars, until I die.*

THINGS TO DO AND THINK ABOUT

Each of the following phrases is an example of one of the visual or aural imagery techniques described above. Match each example to its literary device:

She's as light as a feather	Alliteration
The moonbeams kiss the sea	Onomatopoeia
He's a millstone round her neck	Personification
Your bag weighs a ton	Hyperbole
Splash!	Assonance
Crumbling thunder of seas	Metaphor
Peter Piper picked a peck of pickled peppers	Simile

ONLINE

Now that you know something about the differences between figurative and literal language, you might like to try recognising some figurative items on your own. Before we start practising exam questions, why not ease yourself into the recognition process with a game of Hangman? Try 'Figures of speech' found at www.brightredbooks.net/N5English. Work on your own or with a partner.

ANALYSIS QUESTIONS: IMAGERY

WORKING WITH IMAGERY

It's one thing to know the more common items of figurative language, quite another to be able to recognise them at work and to comment on the effect they create.

SOME PRACTICE QUESTIONS

Here are some which use the visual-imagery techniques from the table on the previous page. Work through these examples on your own, using the table to help you before looking at suggested answers on the Digital Zone. We'll be working on the examples in the right-hand column later.

Johann Hari reflects on a science-fiction novel he has been reading about an imagined world where books have been forgotten:

I have been thinking about this because I recently moved flat, which for me meant boxing and heaving several Everests of books, accumulated obsessively since I was a kid. Ask me to throw away a book, and I begin shaking and insist that I just couldn't bear to part company with it, no matter how unlikely it is I will ever read (say) a 1,000-page biography of little-known Portuguese dictator Antonio Salazar. As I stacked my books high, and watched my friends get buried in landslides of novels, it struck me that this scene might be incomprehensible a generation from now. The book – the physical paper book – is being circled by a shoal of sharks, with sales down 9 percent this year alone. It's being chewed by the e-book. It's being gored by the death of the bookshop and the library.

(Adapted from Johann Hari, 'How to survive in the age of distraction', the *Independent*, 24 June 2011)

(a) Show how the writer's imagery makes clear the number of books he possesses. **2**

(b) How does the writer use imagery to make clear the threat to the paper book? **2**

Chloe Veltman writes about the reaction of the audience to the stage performance of the British singer, Morrissey:

The gladioli are in flight. On the stage of the Henry Fonda Theatre in Hollywood, a slender man in heavy 1950s style eye-glasses, floral shirt, white jeans and pompadour hairdo is energetically hurling a bunch of gangly blooms into the audience whilst singing something about spending warm summer days indoors writing frightening verse to a buck-toothed girl in Luxembourg. In the auditorium, tough-looking twenty-somethings in cuffed jeans, baseball boots and voluminous quiffs sing word-perfectly along, their eyes shining as they strain to catch the somersaulting stems like blushing bridesmaids outside a country church. Gradually, the adoration turns into unabashed devotion, as people try to clamber onto the stage. Those that make it past the heavy-set bouncers cling desperately onto their pop idol like lepers begging for a miracle.

(Chloe Veltman, 'The passion of the Morrissey', in the *Believer*, July–August 2012 Music Issue)

(a) How does the writer use imagery to suggest that the 'tough-looking twenty-somethings' are not as tough as they appear? **2**

(b) Identify and explain the imagery by which Veltman makes clear the strength of the fans' 'devotion'. **2**

contd

Jonathan Thompson takes off on a cycling holiday in the Outer Hebrides but runs into difficulties finding a taxi to get him from the airport to his hotel:

'Don't worry,' says the lady who makes the tea in the arrivals/departures/baggage lounge. 'The Post Office van will take you.' Half an hour later, I'm helping the local post lady, Morag, with her round – bouncing alongside her in the battered red van like a cross between Marty McFly and Jess the Cat. As we drive across the loch-dotted landscape, locals get into and out of the back of the van like human parcels, delivering themselves en route. They chat to each other in their first language, Gaelic, with a few English words – 'carpet' … 'loony' … '90-odd quid' – popping up within the lilting language like remote Atlantic islands.

(Adapted from 'Cycling Scotland's new Hebridean trail', in the *Guardian*, 31 August 2012)

(a) Comment on how the writer uses imagery to show that he does not take his situation too seriously.   **2**

(b) Using your own words, explain fully how the writer continues the idea that passengers were 'like human parcels'.   **2**

(c) Identify the means by which the writer develops the idea that English is not greatly used by the island's Gaelic-speakers.   **2**

ONLINE TEST

For further revision of the use of imagery, test yourself online at www.brightredbooks.net/N5English

THINGS TO DO AND THINK ABOUT

In all of your answers, you will have had to locate the image itself, identify the figurative device in question (simile, metaphor etc.) and then – most importantly of all – look for what links the two things being compared (e.g. a comparison between Mount Everest and a pile of books suggests that the pile of books reaches vast heights, just as Everest does). Once you have done this, you need to explain the effect the image has on you, the reader. So, we might have something like this as an answer to that first question:

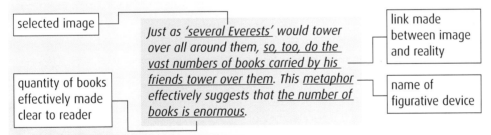

Consider your answers to the previous questions again. Have you fully located, identified and explained the effect of the imagery in each?

ANALYSIS QUESTIONS: WORD CHOICE

DON'T FORGET

The words you will be asked to comment on will usually be ones that are rich in connotations. Be prepared to describe the picture that these connotations create in your imagination.

WORKING WITH WORD CHOICE

Like imagery, **word choice** deals in pictures, too. But this time, the picture is created not in the writer's head but in yours, the reader's.

In other words, word-choice questions exploit the associations which we make with certain words. Often, we do not consciously think about these associations. Word-choice questions, however, will make you do just that. We call these associations in our heads **connotations**.

EXPLORING CONNOTATIONS

Think about the dictionary definition (or **denotation**, if you wish) of *thin*. A dictionary definition might be *having little flesh on the body*. The following words could in certain circumstances be used as possible alternatives, but which of these would you like to be called? What are the connotations of each one? Discuss with a partner or in a group what kind of thinness is suggested by the picture conjured up by each word. Attractive? Unattractive?

scrawny slender lean cadaverous skinny spare underweight svelte slight slim

Verbs, too, can paint pictures, just like adjectives. Consider for a moment the neutral statement:

Blair walked into the room.

'walked' is a neutral word, free of any connotations. But were we to replace 'walked' with any of the following, what would the connotations tell us about the mood, feelings or appearance of Blair?

Discuss with a partner or in a group what you feel the connotations to be.

slouched strode crept skipped waddled

LET'S TRY THAT OUT

Hadley Freeman is appalled by the fact that the wearing of real fur might be making a comeback.

While fur is obviously disgusting, it is also incredibly useful in that it alerts you to the fact that the person wearing it is a complete moron, without you having to waste time talking to them.

('Why you can never look good in a fur coat': Hadley Freeman in the *Guardian*, 6 February 2011)

(a) Show how the writer's word choice alerts you to her contempt for the wearers of fur. **2**

To answer a word-choice question, you need to be on the lookout for words or short expressions that leap out at you as suggesting a colourful attitude to something under discussion. The words chosen will be far from neutral in their effect on readers. So, here we might end up with three possible candidates:

'disgusting' suggests that she looks down on the wearer with scorn.

'(complete) moron' suggests that the wearer is seen as a total idiot by the writer.

'waste (time)' suggests that discussion with the wearer is wholly pointless.

Answering tip: word-choice questions can be answered very directly: select a word, place it in inverted commas and follow it with *suggests/gives the impression that/makes me think of* – then, in your own words, state the associations (or connotations) you have with it.

contd

If you think there might be two words making up a phrase, put the less essential one in brackets.

You do not need to write in full sentences. Avoid phrases longer than two or three words; examiners would then ask which word it is you have actually chosen.

Paddy Woodworth returns to Vietnam to evaluate the developing tourism product that is Phu Quoc.

It's still quite easy to walk alone on an idyllic beach in Phu Quoc, and imagine you are the only person on a pristine island. It's even easier to imagine you are alone if you walk 100 metres into one of the remaining patches of majestic jungle.

But it is not as easy as it was. We first went to this Vietnamese treasure in the Gulf of Thailand five years ago. Already the high-rise hotels on some stretches of the west coast were reminiscent of the worst of the Costa del Sol, with outraged TripAdvisor reviews to match.

This time around, we could see from the plane that many hectares of jungle had been gouged out for a massive international airport in the middle of the island. Unless a few resorts that offer tourists real encounters with Phu Quoc's remarkable environment and culture can turn the tide, the fate of yet another 'paradise island' seems sealed.

In reality, of course, neither the beaches nor the jungle have been truly pristine for a very long time. They have been fished and logged for many centuries, but only recently, and quite abruptly, has their exploitation threatened to become unsustainable. And Phu Quoc has probably never been much of a paradise for its own people, and certainly not over the last century.

During the worst years of the American war (as they understandably remember it here), the South Vietnamese army, allied to the US, established a huge prison camp on the island for NLF insurgents. After the latter's victory in 1975, the new communist authorities turned it into a rather grim museum, billed as one of the top 10 tourist attractions today.

Phu Quoc also saw fierce fighting between the new government and the notorious Khmer Rouge, who claimed it for Cambodia, in the early 1970s. Today the island is at peace, though the rush to development makes life a grim struggle for the poor. The small capital, Duong Dong, boasts markets that offer dazzling cornucopias of local produce: fish, fruit, spices and vegetables of mind-boggling diversity and often – to us at least – startling shapes and colours. The prices also seem rock-bottom to our pockets, but many local people can't afford them.

Wander just 50 metres off the tourist trail, and you will encounter hovels that match anywhere in Asia for abject poverty, in sharp contrast to the often garish McMansions that are springing up along the main roads.

(Paddy Woodworth, 'Paradise found', the *Irish Times*, Saturday 1 September 2012)

(a) Show how the writer's word choice in the first two paragraphs helps us to understand his admiration for the beauties of the island.

2

(b) Show how the word choice in paragraphs three and four expresses the writer's distaste for what is happening to the island.

2

(c) How does the writer use word choice in the last two paragraphs to contrast the attractions and horrors of the island?

2

Here you need to be confident in expressing what image you take away from the writer's selection of vocabulary: for example, *'garish McMansions' makes me think of hideous, brightly coloured buildings that are as alike as any McDonald's hamburgers.*

ONLINE TEST

For more study on how to spot and answer word choice questions, visit www.brightredbooks.net/N5English

THINGS TO DO AND THINK ABOUT

We all carry connotations of words in our heads; it's just a question of digging deep and articulating the image that comes to mind.

ANALYSIS QUESTIONS: PUNCTUATION

WORKING WITH PUNCTUATION

So far in our survey of analysis questions, we have been commenting on how writers make *expression* more vivid within a sentence.

Now we turn to looking at the sentence itself and the features that help shape it: punctuation.

A basic understanding of the contribution of basic punctuation marks to a sentence is essential. The good news is that they are easily mastered. You need to be familiar with the following punctuation marks and, as with other types of analysis questions, be prepared to discuss the <u>effect</u> of their use on the sentence.

Full stop	.	Its position indicates the completion of a sentence. The position of the full stop in a paragraph determines whether we are dealing with long or short sentences. The effect of each we will discuss shortly.
Comma	,	Usually used to separate brief items in a list. *Apples, pears, bananas and a grapefruit.* Used before and after a phrase, commas are said to be used as **parenthesis** markers. *Enter Arthur, a distant cousin, in love with Anne.* The phrase *a distant cousin* is said to be <u>in parenthesis</u>. When answering questions, we say 'The phrase in parenthesis adds additional information about ...'. See also pairs of dashes and brackets below.
Semi-colon	;	Often used to separate larger items in a list. *A beach house in Bermuda; a flat in Paris, on the Champs Elysées no less; a chalet in the Alps; a castle in Scotland with over 40 rooms: all these were owned by their aunt.* They also indicate a turning point in a balanced sentence. *Sober, he was unpredictable; drunk, he was dangerous. To err is human; to forgive divine.*
Colon	:	A colon may signal an explanation or elaboration that is to follow. *It was now night: stars twinkled overhead and the moon was rising.* Or it may signal an upcoming quotation. *Criticised for being harsh, Les replies: 'Heart like a flint, that's me.'* It may also introduce a list. *Her garden was a picture: marigolds, lupins, roses, daisies and, in spring, masses of tulips.*
Dashes and brackets	– – ( )	Pairs of dashes, brackets or commas on either side of a phrase – *her mother's cousin* – are used to create what we call a phrase *in parenthesis*. When answering questions, we say 'The phrase in parenthesis adds additional information about ...'. An individual dash can be used to add emphasis or importance to a word or phrase following it. *And there it lay before them, glittering in the blue Aegean – Hydra.* An individual dash can sometimes also be used as a kind of informal colon, indicating a concluding list or explanation. *He had taken great trouble over their evening meal – prawns, roast venison and a fine raspberry tart.*
Ellipsis	...	In mid-sentence, these three dots can be used to suggest an interruption, hesitation or indecision. Used at the end of the sentence, they can suggest anticipation or suspense. *The door opened and a hand appeared ...*
Exclamation mark	!	Usually used to indicate strong emotion on the part of the writer: often surprise, excitement or anger. *It was Bill!*

contd

DON'T FORGET

If a question asks you to comment on sentence structure, the first thing to do is check out the sentence to see if any of the above punctuation marks could be the basis of your answer. It might be as simple as that. But make sure you say what the effect of the punctuation is.

Question mark	**?**	To indicate a question, which may be a structuring device for that section of the article – i.e. the writer asks a question and then proceeds to answer it in the following paragraph. A series of questions may well be there to signal the writer's confusion or bewilderment. *Who could she turn to? Was there anyone she could trust? What if they were all against her?* Sometimes this can mark the end of a rhetorical question, which invites readers to share the writer's views. *What kind of society turns its back on those in need?* You need to say precisely what the apparent aim of the writer is: for example, 'to win the reader's support <u>for his views on what constitutes a just society</u>'.
Inverted commas (quotation marks)	**' '**	Around an individual word or phrase, inverted commas suggest that the writer is casting doubt on the surface meaning of the word. *I had little faith in the 'help' being offered by the bank.* Here the writer is indicating that the 'help' is so-called help, rather than real assistance. Quotation marks are also used to indicate the title of a poem, a song, an article or a chapter in a book. (The title of a book, a film or a play is indicated in print by italics, but in handwriting you would use underlining or perhaps quotation marks.)

THINGS TO DO AND THINK ABOUT

If a question invites you to comment on the writer's language, as it often will do, you can point to all sorts of things: imagery, sentence structure, tone or word choice – but don't overlook punctuation. By all means, talk about these other aspects; but, if you are stuck for a comment, examine the passage's punctuation and its effect on shaping the writer's meaning. This could be the means of picking up a valuable mark or two.

ANALYSIS QUESTIONS: SENTENCE STRUCTURE

Now, while a good writer can make a sentence do almost anything, the sentences on whose structure you will be asked to comment tend to fall into certain recurring categories. Again, it is the *effect* of these sentence-structure choices which the writer has made that you will be asked to comment on.

WORKING WITH SENTENCE STRUCTURE

You have just learned all about different types of punctuation that you are likely to encounter in your Close Reading. The chances are, however, that you will need to discuss punctuation in combination with some of the sentence features discussed below. So, what might you expect to be asked about? Here are some strong possibilities.

Long sentences	Used to suggest the sheer length of something, a route of a river or road, for example, or the complexity of a process, or the boredom of something dragging on and on.
Short sentences	Used to intensify the impact/drama of what is being said. A brief remark in a sentence of its own gains greatly in dramatic effect.
	And with that, she left.
	Any form of persuasive writing, such as advertising, may well make use of the short sentence.
	Try it. You'll love it. Every woman does.
	Be very alert to the power of the short sentence after a particularly long one: the dramatic impact is increased even more.
A list (neutral, with climax or anti-climax)	Used to underline/emphasise/highlight the sheer number of items, actions or people being described.
	Always check lists out for additional possibilities. It might build to a **climax** –
	She had played hostess to generals, princes, kings and even the mighty Napoleon himself
	– a technique which adds to the impact of the final item.
	It might, however, end in an **anti-climax** –
	His case contained a pair of Gucci loafers, a Rolex watch, cologne by Chanel and a pair of dirty underpants
	– a technique which is usually used for humorous effect.
	Of course, it might simply be a neutral list! But it's a sound idea to check out any list for climax or anti-climax.
Sentences without verbs	These are known as minor sentences. Sometimes they create a chatty, informal effect.
	Great! Another fine mess. What next?
	Or they can function like the short sentences described above: to add dramatic impact.
	A woman's glove. Slightly blood-stained.

contd

Inverted word order	Normal word order in English tends to follow this pattern:
	He was fierce in his claim to innocence.
	But, to emphasise/underline/highlight a certain element in the sentence, we can invert the normal order, usually to place the important word(s) first. So, we get
	Fierce he was in his claim to innocence.
	But the inversion can also be manipulated to place the important word to be emphasised at the end, thus giving
	In his claim to innocence he was fierce.
	Exam tip: if you cannot see anything at all in a sentence to comment on, check out inversion. It is often one of the last things we think of. And it *might* just be the right answer!
Repetition	This may take the form of repeated words or phrases to underline/intensify the idea the writer is seeking to emphasise at a particular point.
	A good cyclist needs ... A good cyclist hopes that ... But a good cyclist knows above all that ...
	Note that these repetitions in the closing stages of a text might be building to a climax. It is worth mentioning in your answer if you detect this.
Balanced sentences	When writers wish to make us strongly aware of some contrast that they want to indicate, they sometimes resort to these. They are recognisable by the semi-colon (;) that acts as a pivot, or balancing point, in the middle of the sentence.
	Alive, she had been seen as a saint; dead, she was quickly demonised.
Rhetorical question	These are questions expecting no direct answer, rather the reader's support for the writer's views.
	Who wants to see a child suffer in this way?
	Here the reader is expected to share the writer's horror at the ill-treatment of children.
Parallel structures	These are patterns of either phrases or words which give a pleasing predictability and rhythm to the sentence. The effect is to add emphasis to what is being said.
	It is by logic we prove, but by intuition we discover (da Vinci).
	The ants were everywhere: climbing *over jampots,* swarming *under the sink,* scrambling *into cupboards,* diving *into the bin.*
	The likeness of pattern here (verb + preposition) makes for a more memorable phrase and creates a greater impact than a less patterned structure would.

 THINGS TO DO AND THINK ABOUT

Find and read an article from the Comment section of a respected newspaper, either in print or online, and analyse the punctuation and sentence structure used throughout the piece. Remember to use the highlighting technique mentioned earlier in this chapter. Did you notice any of the techniques mentioned above being used? To what effect?

ANALYSIS QUESTIONS: PUNCTUATION AND SENTENCE STRUCTURE COMBINED

When faced with a question about sentence structure, remember that it is extremely difficult to draw a hard line between sentence structure and punctuation. You should be alert to the fact that mention of a feature of one might lead you into a discussion of the other. This can only enrich your answer. And remember, there is a limited number of possibilities in answers of this type; so make sure you know all of them well in advance of the exam.

LET'S TRY THIS OUT – 'A TIME BEST FORGOTTEN'

DON'T FORGET

As with other analysis questions, questions asking you to look at sentence structure or punctuation will expect you to say what effect a particular sentence feature has on the reader. That does not mean generalising; it means spelling out how that particular feature works in that particular sentence. So, an answer might look like this: *The writer uses **parallel structures** to say the ants were everywhere: 'climbing over jam pots, swarming under the sink, scrambling into cupboards, diving into the bin'. The likeness of pattern here (verb + preposition) creates the idea that the ants were busy getting absolutely everywhere, completely invading the kitchen.* Don't just quote your notes and say 'The parallel structures create a memorable phrase and a greater impact than a less patterned structure would'. You <u>must</u> relate the feature to the actual context in front of you.

It might have been decades ago, but I remember the anguish of that first day as if it were yesterday. I remember the howling when my mum left me with Mrs Bell. I remember the strange looks the other kids gave me when I was at last coaxed into the classroom. Other people remember, too, and any time I meet up with them, they never let me forget this.

I remember it all: the seemingly vast building, the coal-fired stove, the 'large' pupils in primary 2, the honky-tonk tinkling of the piano, the endless school day, walking home in the winter dark. A time best forgotten.

(a) Show how the writer's sentence structure in paragraph one emphasises the point being made about unhappy experiences.　　2

(b) Show how the writer uses sentence structure in paragraph two to draw attention to the power of memory.　　2

(c) How does the writer use sentence structure in paragraph two to underline the unhappiness of that early time?　　2

(d) Explain how the writer's language shows that his memory of the Primary 2 pupils might not have been quite accurate.　　2

LET'S TRY THIS OUT – 'THE PERILS OF OPTIMISM'

The fitness culture is everywhere. Think about how often we run into sweaty bodies in lycra – some decidedly unappealing in this most unforgiving of materials – when trying to negotiate our way home from work. Think of the number of times fit young men and women look out at us from media advertising exhorting us to buy such and such a health-giving product. Think of the times we look sadly at our expanding waistlines and begin to wonder if perhaps it is not too late to do something about it. In pessimistic moods, such reflections are depressing; in optimistic moods, they're downright dangerous.

(a) Suggest two ways in which the writer here uses sentence structure to underline the points he is making about what he sees as our obsession with fitness. **4**

(b) What purpose do the dashes serve in sentence two? **2**

Appearing in court to give evidence, Cluny seemed to Usher to be a very different man from the sad man he'd seen two weeks before in his office: alert, youthful-looking, enjoying himself mightily. From the dock, Anderson looked on sneeringly, as if Cluny's treachery was just another harsh lesson in the wicked ways of fate in his life. And life is what he got.

(a) Show how the writer uses sentence structure to emphasise how appearing in court had changed Cluny. **2**

(b) How does the writer's sentence structure bring out the severity of the sentence? **2**

Fiona had never cared for the Festival: traffic, never exactly free-flowing, came to an almost dead stop; tourists seemed to clog up all the pavements; her friends took off for all points of the compass; she could never get into her favourite restaurants; the infernal din of the Tattoo kept her awake for hours; there was always the feeling that she was about to have her pockets picked; and this morning there was a dead man in her front garden.

'I'm not sure how to say this,' she explained to the police when her shock allowed her to get to the phone, 'but when I went out this morning, there was … I found … well, he was … dead.'

(a) Show how the writer's sentence structure adds impact in paragraph one. **3**

(b) How does the writer use sentence structure to convey the girl's state of mind in paragraph two? **2**

ONLINE TEST

For more practice at identifying sentence structure and punctuation use, test yourself at www.brightredbooks.net/N5English

THINGS TO DO AND THINK ABOUT

What have we learned here? Firstly, you really have to know the function of the various punctuation marks and the possible choices available to writers when considering sentence structure. Secondly, you will not impress examiners if you simply identify the writer's selected feature(s). You must say what its *effect* is on the reader.

ANALYSIS QUESTIONS: TONE

WORKING WITH QUESTIONS ABOUT TONE

Our ears are quick to detect tone in conversation. We can hear quite well when people are being, say, chatty or humorous or persuasive or emotive or ironic or matter-of-fact. Facial expressions and body language help spell this out. But trying to pin down the tone in a written piece of text can be more tricky. One writer has called tone 'the unspoken attitude of the author to his subject and/or audience'. We need to look for clues or markers in the text which help us to make out what this 'unspoken attitude' might be.

Writers can create tone by a whole variety of means, but here are some clues to determining tone.

TONE	MARKERS	INTENDED EFFECT
Chatty/informal/ colloquial	• Short sentences • Abbreviations: *can't, it'll, won't* • Free use of first/second-person pronouns: *I, you* • Chatty expressions: *Come on! Right on! No problem.* • Free use of exclamation and question marks. • Sentences without a verb. (Minor sentences.) *No change there then.* • Slang expressions: *Back in a jiffy, a smack on the gob* • Informal commands: *Go early ... Take a picnic ... Stay away from ...*	To get persuasively closer to the reader, giving the effect of someone chatting informally to his/her friends.
Humorous	• Use of exaggeration or a series of exaggerations (also called hyperbole): *He was so thin I've seen more fat on a chip!* • Telling jokes/stories against the speaker or topic • Mixing formal and informal styles: *Please refrain from asking for credit as a smack on the gob frequently offends.*	To strive for comic effect, sometimes simply to amuse, but sometimes to underline and mock the absurd/pointless nature of some issue under discussion.

contd

TONE	MARKERS	INTENDED EFFECT
Emotive	• Use of words which stir up strong emotions such as anger or pity: *weary pensioner, helpless infant, heartless thieves, terrified for their lives*	To arouse extremes of feeling in the face of fear, suffering, injustice, loneliness or cruelty.
Ironic/tongue-in-cheek	• Often saying the opposite of what you mean: *The concert lasts four hours? With no interval? How lovely!*	To criticise or mock something or somebody in a humorous way to make a critical point.
Persuasive	• Using comparatives/superlatives: *A better way of banking, the best in its class, the newest sat-nav* • Words highlighting excellence: *quality, perfection, integrity* • Words suggesting trustworthiness: *for generations, the choice of experts* • Rhetorical questions: *What kind of parent sends a child to school hungry?*	To win over readers to author's point of view/beliefs.
Factual/Matter-of-fact	• Usually created by a series of statements which avoid any of the above slanting of information. *Comets are more common than is popularly imagined. Astronomers believe that as many as one trillion could exist in the farther reaches of the solar system. Best known of all is Halley's Comet.*	To impart information in a neutral, unemotional manner. Sometimes used effectively to contrast with the more colourful tones described above.

Tracking down answers to questions on tone can sometimes cause candidates difficulties. Clues can sometimes be at hand by checking the introduction at the beginning of the article. The heading information here may point you in the right direction. 'Johann Hari takes a light-hearted look at …' Or there may be questions which find you referring to persuasive word choice, **irony** or emotive imagery in your answers. Does the writer continue in this manner?

You will need evidence to back up your choice of tone, as you would with any other analysis question, so make sure you have more than one item of evidence to offer the examiner. That means knowing all the possibilities mentioned in the tone grid here. And be familiar with all the giveaway markers long before you go into the exam room!

ONLINE TEST

For more practice at identifying tone, test yourself at www. brightredbooks.net/N5English

THINGS TO DO AND THINK ABOUT

To help you check out how well you have absorbed tonal markers, try out this activity. The tone markers you have studied in the grid will help you here. For each of the following, identify both the tone and all the tonal markers that helped you arrive at your answer.

1. And there I was banging on about my cash problems and her with a Heinz beans box to doss down in. Nuff said. Sign of the times.

2. Bring three pieces of identity with you, a letter of recommendation from your headteacher, a full CV, the form filled-in in triplicate and a cheque for £150. You have to admit it, they don't ask much.

3. Wearily, she laid the Asda bag down on the park bench, grateful that she was at least half-way home. Would she make the last gruelling mile, she asked herself? Hauling her frail form up from the bench, she tottered unsteadily on.

4. With more than 75 years in the travel business, we pride ourselves on our standing in the industry. 75 years of returning customers point to a service which is second-to-none. A reputation like ours is hard to come by, that's why we go the extra mile to ensure that our customers keep coming back. With us, many happy returns are not just for birthdays!

5. The last time I saw legs that thin, there was a message tied round them. And talking of pigeons, his chest was so convex I fully expected to see feathers on it.

THE READING-SKILLS FAMILY: THE EVALUATION QUESTION

WORKING WITH EVALUATION QUESTIONS

Those questions may come towards the end of the series of questions. And there is a good reason for this late positioning. For some of the material you may have noted in answering understanding and analysis questions could be useful again here.

Be careful, however. It is never a question of simply repeating what you have said earlier. It will usually mean taking that earlier material and moving it one stage further. In other words, what is your opinion of how well the writer has used a technique, a way of illustrating a point or structuring a conclusion?

APPROACHES TO EVALUATION

Here you have to be prepared to have an opinion of your own. Beware, however, of giving some generalised waffle.

You also need to bear in mind that the text was chosen by the examiners for its excellence of expression. But it's your task to point out and give your opinion of how well writers achieve particular effects.

EVALUATING TECHNIQUES

Evaluation questions may vary quite a lot in their wording:

Show how an aspect of ... conveys the writer's sense of ...

Refer to an example of word choice or imagery.

Explain why the writer's use of ... is effective in advancing his point.

Explain why the expression ... effectively illustrates our relationship with ...

Why is it appropriate to introduce ... with the expression ...?

Identify by example a technique used to convey ... and comment on its effectiveness.

You will note that you are often asked to say how *effective* a technique is in *conveying* the writer's sense of *wonder, delight, surprise, irritation, amusement* or some such response in a certain area of the text.

So, what do you do?

1 Locate certain items from the text: highlighting is again a good idea.

2 Identify aspects of style at work, for example simile, personification, list, anecdote, ironic tone, word choice.

3 Explain in your own words the effect this item is having on readers.

4 Evaluate in your own words the effectiveness of this item in getting the writer's point across.

Yes, you've noted there are similarities in the above steps with what you are expected to do in analysis answers. Why? Well, it's difficult to evaluate something before you have said how it works. So, for your evaluation answer, you need to pick out your chosen item for comment, identify it, explain how it affects the reader and only then say how well you think it is doing its job in the text.

contd

DON'T FORGET

Do not hide behind technical terms when answering evaluation questions. Yes, you need technical terms, but, even more, you need a well-expressed opinion of your own about how well your selected technique for comment is performing its task in the text.

ONLINE

Check out some great book reviews online through the '*Guardian*: books and reviews' link at www.brightredbooks. net/N5English for some professional evaluations of literature.

DON'T FORGET

Usually, the writing you are being asked to comment on has been chosen for its excellence in the eyes of the person setting the paper. If, however, you wish to make a negative evaluative comment on some point, you are perfectly at liberty to do so. But be very careful. You will need to back up your comment with convincing evidence from the text and a soundly argued case. An exam is no place to air private prejudices.

So, what would the answer to an Evaluation question look like? No two answers will ever be alike, but the following makes a suggestion of how to apply the information from the steps above.

Suppose the passage had been about a road race passing the writer's window with the following question:

Referring in detail to two techniques employed in the passage, suggest why the writer is effective in conveying the humour of the situation.   4

One possible answer might be, say:

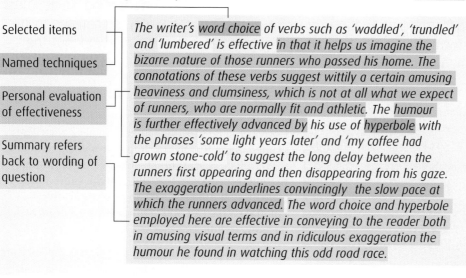

Selected items

Named techniques

Personal evaluation of effectiveness

Summary refers back to wording of question

The writer's word choice of verbs such as 'waddled', 'trundled' and 'lumbered' is effective in that it helps us imagine the bizarre nature of those runners who passed his home. The connotations of these verbs suggest wittily a certain amusing heaviness and clumsiness, which is not at all what we expect of runners, who are normally fit and athletic. The humour is further effectively advanced by his use of hyperbole with the phrases 'some light years later' and 'my coffee had grown stone-cold' to suggest the long delay between the runners first appearing and then disappearing from his gaze. The exaggeration underlines convincingly the slow pace at which the runners advanced. The word choice and hyperbole employed here are effective in conveying to the reader both in amusing visual terms and in ridiculous exaggeration the humour he found in watching this odd road race.

DON'T FORGET

Your answer to an evaluation question will often reuse material you have used for an earlier answer. The difference is: now you have to give your opinion on how well it does its job. Watch out! Sometimes it allows you a free choice on what you pick out for comment; sometimes it may specify particular items (word choice, sentence structure etc.).

EVALUATING CONCLUSIONS

A popular evaluation question is often to ask you to say how *effective* or *appropriate* or *fitting* you find the conclusion *to the passage as a whole*.

This involves you in a quick mental survey of your reading of the full passage.

Then ask yourself the following questions:

1   Does the conclusion **revisit** the points which have been covered in the rest of the article? If it does, you need to say something like *In revisiting the fact that ..., the fact that ... and the mention of ..., the writer is pulling together the main ideas from earlier in her article and effectively reminding us of her key arguments in the article as a whole. By doing this, the writer is providing an effective and satisfying sense of completion to the passage.*

2   Does some wording in the conclusion **connect** with a statement or phrase used in the introduction or much earlier in the passage? If it does, use terms along the lines of *The reference to ... in the concluding lines reminds us of a similar phrase in the first paragraph when he suggests that ... This return to an earlier idea in the conclusion gives a satisfying cyclical feel/arrives back at a point from where we started/connects back to the starting point in a way which makes us feel the topic has been explored fully/which brings us back, but now with a fuller understanding, to the earlier comment.*

3   Does it both **revisit** and **connect**? This is a popular structuring technique with fine journalists and writers. Do not be surprised if you feel you need to make reference to both techniques and comment appropriately from both 1 and 2.

ONLINE TEST

Practise some more evaluation questions online at www.brightredbooks.net/N5English.

THINGS TO DO AND THINK ABOUT

As you begin to read the text, glance quickly at the questions to see if there are any questions towards the end which may indicate some kind of evaluation of the text as a whole. With the question(s) at the back of your mind as you read, you may be saving yourself some time at the end of the paper when you come to reflect on the points to be evaluated.

THE READING-SKILLS FAMILY: THE INFERENCE-MAKING QUESTION

These are broader questions in that they ask you to look below the surface of the text – or between the lines, so to speak – to seek out what the writer is getting at, but not saying directly. You will need to look for clues to help you work out the writer's underlying meaning. Sometimes you are being asked to infer the true **feelings** or **point of view** of the writer; sometimes to infer the precise nature of **information** which has only been hinted at; sometimes to work out the **emotions** of a person mentioned in the text.

INFERRING THE AUTHOR'S MEANING

How do you do this? Well, there will have been clues planted in the text by the author. It is your job to look for the clues. Sometimes it is the **accumulation of factual information** that will give the game away; sometimes it will be **word choice** or **figurative language** which let you in on the writer's deeper meaning or intentions.

You are being asked to work quite hard to gather your information – and the higher marks will reflect this. Be sure to answer them in sufficient detail to collect all the available marks.

EXAMPLE:

Let's take a look at an example of how to track down answers to inference-making questions.

Glancing at his watch as he drove north on the Paris–Brussels motorway, Hamish saw he had loads of time before the Zeebrugge–Hull ferry sailed. His first brush with chateau life in northern France had been an eye-opener for him. He had not expected Celine's family to be quite so rich. The antiques everywhere, the tapestries in nearly every room, the quietly spoken servants. They certainly lived well. Chateau life at Pierrefonds was decidedly different from home in Newtongrange. And then there was Celine's strange confession. Sweeping up the map of northern France on the passenger seat, he slapped it smartly into the glovebox and pressed his foot down hard on the accelerator.

How likely, in your opinion, is it that Hamish will make a second visit to Pierrefonds? Give evidence from this paragraph to support your answer.

4

ONLINE

For more on inference, check out: 'BBC Bitesize: Inference Questions' at www.brightredbooks.net/N5English.

contd

ANSWER:

To answer this inference-making question, you will need to make use of the Close Reading skills you have been acquiring. What, then, might be of interest to us here as we try to work out what the writer is implying about Hamish's reaction to Pierrefonds and the likelihood of a second visit?

- **Understanding skills.** We need to study accumulated factual information. Look at how little pressured by time Hamish is – and then examine his driving behaviour.
- **Analysis skills.** There are some examples of word choice which give us a clue as to what the writer is implying.

From these clues, our answer might read:

- *A second visit to Pierrefonds seems unlikely.*
- *Although he was very early for the ferry ('loads of time'), he sets off at a great pace ('pressed his foot down hard on the accelerator'), which suggests he was keen to put the visit speedily behind him.*
- *'sweeping up' suggests that he wanted to be rid of the local map rather urgently (although, being far from home, he might be expected to find it useful).*
- *'slapped it smartly' suggests that, after reflecting on the visit, he wanted any reminder of his trip out of his sight once and for all.*

LET'S TRY THAT OUT

Now try for yourself this extract from a newspaper review of a new single from the veteran singer David Bowie. The writer examines the general reaction of the press to its release. Two clues to start you off:

- Check out the factual information you gather in the first and last paragraphs. Do you see any contrasts or contradictions here?
- Check out word choice or imagery you find in the extract. What connotations or associations do some of the most colourful expressions carry?

> *David Bowie is a genius, but not even a fan like me could claim it was his greatest work. Yet he has been hosed down with the kind of hosannas usually lavished on grandpa when he manages to totter to the potting shed all by himself.*
>
> *I think even Bowie might be embarrassed by the reaction to what, by a long margin, is not his best work.*
>
> *Still, in the finest British tradition, he'll be bracing himself for the inevitable backlash when the album comes out later this year.*

(Jan Moir, 'Bowie ballyhoo that's enough to make a laughing gnome weep!', *Daily Mail*, 11 January 2013)

What view of the British press is implied by Jan Moir here?   3

ONLINE TEST

For more practice at inference questions, test yourself online at www.brightredbooks.net/N5English.

ONLINE

How did you get on? Visit www.brightredbooks.net/N5English for a suggested answer.

THINGS TO DO AND THINK ABOUT

Inference-making questions build on the understanding and analysis skills you have already been acquiring in Close Reading. Be particularly alert to the accumulation of factual information which does not quite add up. Use, too, your analysis skills to examine word choice or figurative language to work out for yourself why these particular examples have been selected and what you think they are being used to hint at indirectly.

THE READING-SKILLS FAMILY: THE SUMMARISING QUESTION

Once again, we come upon a question-type which, like understanding questions, tests your vocabulary and ability to pinpoint key information concisely.

Just as 'lifting' words and expressions in understanding questions is to be avoided, so, too, is it in summarising ones. Additionally, you will need to take stretches of the text in question and reduce it to its essential message, cutting out interesting but non-essential detail. That's the real challenge, perhaps: making up your mind what to remove. Then, in your own words, you have to summarise as briefly as possible what remains.

LET'S TRY THAT OUT

In many ways, you face here the same challenges as understanding questions pose: finding your own words to express the writer's ideas – but this time as economically as possible. Let's try working an example together.

EXAMPLE:

Here is an interview with writer Michael Morpurgo, author of more than 100 books for young people, discussing the need to talk to children about the world as it is, no matter how grisly.

> Morpurgo is adamant about darkness being a necessary component of children's literature. 'Our great problem', he explains, 'is that children now know whatever they want to know – at the press of a button they can discover all horrors of the adult world.'
>
> He adds: 'They know very early on that the world is sometimes a very dark, difficult and complex place, and the literature they read must reflect that. Otherwise we're just entertaining them to pass the time. And what's the point? Let them watch television if that's all there is to literature.'

(Hermione Hoby, 'Hay Festival 2011: Michael Morpurgo interview', *Daily Telegraph*, 30 May 2011)

In your own words, explain fully why Morpurgo sees that it is 'necessary' for children's literature to tackle 'darkness'.　　**4**

First, we need to decide what the key ideas are. But we can't just 'lift' them; we need to paraphrase them into our own words. We also need to reduce them to their essentials. And, in a summary, we have no room for phrases like 'at the press of a button' or 'a dark, difficult and complex place'. These are too detailed, as well as not being our own!

Let's take it a step at a time: what are the key ideas of the first section? And can we eventually paraphrase them into our own expressions in brief bullet points, rather than take just individual words? Let's see.

How about saying 'Morpurgo insists that ...'?

Morpurgo ... adamant ... darkness ... necessary component ... children's literature

How about saying 'Through television ...'?

Problem ... at the touch of a button ... discover ... all horrors of the adult world

That would seem to give us two bullet points:

● Morpurgo insists that evil must be included in children's novels.

● Through television, they quickly discover the many nastinesses of grown-up life.

contd

DON'T FORGET

Learning to summarise effectively is essential for performing successfully in the N5 English exam. Summarising, however, is a life skill which will prove useful well beyond N5 English. At college, university or in a commercial workplace, you will find the ability to reduce complex information to its essentials a skill you will need time and again. Master it now.

ONLINE

Read the full interview, 'Hay Festival 2011: Michael Morpurgo interview' online at www.brightredbooks.net/N5English.

Now, using the same technique, see what you get with the second part of the extract.

- What they read has to engage with these problems.

- If it doesn't do so, it is no more serious than television.

EXAMPLE:

Now try this example of summarising on your own. If you get stuck, you will find a suggested answer on the BrightRED Digital Zone. It describes how Scottish novelist Ian Rankin's *Black & Blue* marked a change in the author's approach to fiction-writing.

'Black & Blue' marked more than a commercial breakthrough, however, for many of the novels which followed manifested not only a newly found density and complexity of plot-lines but a keener awareness of contemporary social issues. Admittedly, this had been present before in Rankin's output, as for example, in 'Mortal Causes' (1994) where sectarianism and paramilitary activities were important elements in the plot but in 'Black & Blue' the moral and social issues connected with the de-commissioning of North Sea oil-platforms may be seen to be becoming more all-embracing of the novel's life.

In your own words, explain fully how *Black & Blue* was a 'breakthrough' in Rankin's fiction.　　**4**

THINGS TO DO AND THINK ABOUT

In summarising, avoid **figurative language** of all kinds: metaphors, similes and so on. Avoid also **examples**, **lists**, **comparisons** and any **details of secondary importance**. As in understanding questions, concentrate on using your own words and on **reducing ideas to their essentials**, not just reducing the number of individual words. Try to vary your sentence structure from that of the original; it will lead you away from being tempted to use features from the original too closely.

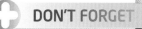

ONLINE TEST

For more practice on summarising questions, test yourself online at www.brightredbooks.net/N5English.

DON'T FORGET

The wider your vocabulary, the easier you'll find it to summarise in your own words. So, if you're not already doing so, get reading quality texts of all kinds!

THE CRITICAL ESSAY: WAYS OF SUCCEEDING

READING THE QUESTION

First, a word of reassurance: you already know more about writing successful critical essays than you might perhaps suspect. How so? Well, in your Close Reading study, you have learned that success is based on being able to understand, analyse and evaluate. Put differently, the skills you learned for coping with those questions will again stand you in good stead when it comes to constructing the body paragraphs of your essays. Just how that's done, you'll see shortly.

To these skills, you will need to add the ability to plan the sequencing of these paragraphs to give your essay a logical progress. You will also need to learn how to frame these body paragraphs with a convincing introduction and conclusion.

But, before we get to the writing stages, we need to learn how to approach the questions themselves.

ONLINE

Have a look at the definitions of question terms which may come up in your exam paper by clicking on 'Essay Zone: Help with Understanding Essay Questions: 21 Terms and Phrases Explained' at www.brightredbooks.net/N5English

DON'T FORGET

Success starts with selecting only material that answers your chosen question. No marks for showing off all your knowledge of the text!

WHAT IS BEING ASKED?

Success starts with fully understanding what the question is getting at and providing an appropriate answer.

A good answer does not tell the examiner everything you have learned about a text.

A good answer selects from your information bank only the information to answer the question in front of you.

That means you may come out of the exam room having used only a percentage of your total knowledge. Frustrating, yes, but if you have selected the correct percentage, you will do well.

THE SELECTION PROCESS

Choosing the correct question is the first key to success. To choose wisely, you will need to know your texts in depth. That means many readings on your own, not just the reading you have done with your teacher in class. Only with that depth of knowledge will you be able to select or reject questions without undue delay. You simply will not have the time to sit pondering tranquilly whether your play, poems or prose work matches up to the demands of the question or not. Decisions need to be made fairly promptly, but not casually. Hence your grasp of the texts must be total.

Once you have decided you have sufficient information to settle on a question, begin by reading the question carefully and underlining or highlighting what you think are key words.

> ### EXAMPLE:
>
> For instance, you may select a question like this:
>
> **Choose a short story or novel in which setting figures prominently.**
>
> **Describe the contribution of the setting and then show how this feature helped your understanding of the text as a whole.**
>
> Underline the words that are pointing you to what the essay will be about. In this case, the words will probably be *setting figures prominently*. In the second line, you will also probably have underlined *Describe the contribution*. Notice, however, that there is a second part to the question:

contd

... and then show how this feature helped your understanding of the text as a whole.

In exam questions at this level, you must always be ready for this second part to the question. Under all the pressure to write down the full details of the setting, you mustn't lose sight of that significant later part of the question. Leave yourself short of time for that, and you will be throwing away vital marks.

So, in your planning, remember to include a section which will deal with this second part.

Critical essay-writing builds on Close Reading skills of the kind we have already discussed in this Study Guide. You need to convince the examiner of your ability to understand, analyse and evaluate in the central section of your essay, just as you did in your Close Reading answers. In Close Reading, you have also explored key elements which make up a good conclusion. The only really new element in critical essay-writing is learning how to construct an impressive introduction. That we shall return to soon.

ONLINE TEST

For more practice on reading the question, test yourself online at www.brightredbooks.net/N5English

DON'T FORGET

Exam questions at this level are usually in two parts. You MUST engage with this second part just as much as the first part.

THINGS TO DO AND THINK ABOUT

Consider the following question:

Choose a poem which arouses strong emotion in you.

Describe how you feel about the poem, and explain how the poet leads you to feel this way.

How do the words in the question help you to understand how you should answer? Which two things does the question ask you to do? Highlight the parts of this question that would shape your essay.

PLANNING A RESPONSE

THE IMPORTANCE OF A PLAN

A plan is necessary for two people: you and the examiner. Start writing without a plan, and you risk going off task and ending up not answering the question. Consequently, you sell yourself short and do not make best use of your information. Similarly, the examiner ends up wondering what on earth you're getting at and marks you down accordingly – to be avoided!

Everyone has his or her own way of planning an essay. Some make lists of points they want to include and link them to particular characters or situations. Some like to draw mind-maps like this one.

Robert Louis Stevenson's *The Strange Case of Dr Jekyll and Mr Hyde* would suit the question below perfectly. So, what would our mind-map look like?

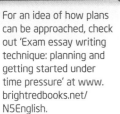

ONLINE

For an idea of how plans can be approached, check out 'Exam essay writing technique: planning and getting started under time pressure' at www.brightredbooks.net/N5English.

ONLINE

Create your own mind-map online! Go to www.brightredbooks.net/N5English.

DON'T FORGET

These mind-map quotations and comments are your first thoughts. You may decide to eliminate some of them for various reasons: lack of time or of relevance to the question, for example. That's fine! It shows you're thinking like a professional writer.

Point 1:
sordid and attractive mixed up in opening description

… the street shone out in contrast to its dingy neighbours, like a fire in a forest.

… freshly painted shutters, well-polished brasses, and general cleanliness and gaiety of note …

BUT … a certain sinister block of building thrust forward its gable on the street.

… and bore in every feature the marks of prolonged and sordid negligence.

The door […] was blistered and distained. Tramps slouched in the recess …

Point 2:
direct linking of Dr Jekyll's handsome home to this sordid building

Round the corner from the by street there was a square of ancient, handsome houses, now for the most part decayed from their high estate.

One house wore a great air of wealth and comfort …

Question: why does Stevenson link them? Making a point about duality? Respectable Jekyll's connection to the sordid?

Choose a short story or novel in which setting figures prominently.

Describe the contribution of the setting and then show how this feature helped your understanding of the text as a whole.

Point 4:
Author combines both attractive and sordid physical setting with darkness and fog

Question: why? To suggest Stevenson's belief in duality of human nature? To set up appropriate, atmospheric setting to explore the darker, concealed aspects of human nature?

Point 3:
key events take place at night/in fog

I was coming home from some place at the end of the world, about three o'clock of a black winter morning … (Hyde's attack on child)

Utterson first encounters Hyde at night

Danvers Carew is murdered at night

A great-coloured pall lowered over heaven …

… and the next moment the fog settled down again upon that part, as brown as umber and cut him off from his blackguardly surroundings.

Question: why darkness and fog? Night mirrors darkness of J's intentions? Fog aids concealment, used literally and metaphorically?

Once you have selected – by whatever planning method – the information which you believe needs to be included, you need to start grouping it into different areas, each one of which might form the basis of a section of your essay.

OPENING STATEMENTS

Whatever approach you take to planning and then to grouping, you must make sure that your plan contains enough evidence to back up the points you want to make. So, it might be a good idea to jot down beside each point a quotation or two which would back up that particular point.

Then, using the ideas linking your group, start to try to word what your opening statement in each section might be. List them one under another. When you list your statements like this, you are in fact writing out an outline essay.

Read this list, and you see at once the line of thought your essay is going to take. Doing this will help to keep you on task; it will also help you to judge your time; and your examiner will be able to follow your train of thought successfully. This way, everyone gains.

So, suppose we were to sort out a sequence of statements from our mind-map, we might end up with something like this:

Statement 1: *In the opening chapter, Stevenson goes to great trouble to establish that the area around Hyde's laboratory home presents a setting which is a curious mixture of the prosperous and the dingy.*

Statement 2: *There is yet a further contrast of environments, for we later learn that this squalid laboratory building is connected to buildings in a nearby square. The puzzle grows as to why Stevenson has deliberately linked them.*

Statement 3: *The setting is enriched even more by having the key moments in the story take place at night.*

Statement 4: *Weather, too, backs up the mood of the piece in key incidents.*

STATEMENTS: STEERING YOUR ESSAY TO SUCCESS

Before we go any further, let's take a look at what we mean by statements in this context. For essay purposes, we perhaps need to broaden our definition of statement. It can be a single utterance, but it can also be more than one. Have a look back at *Statement 2*. In this statement, *the agenda is set out for what is going to be discussed in the rest of the paragraph.* In other words, it lays out the basis for your *understanding* of a main point that is to be made. And you will remember from your Close Reading work that answers to understanding questions do just that: they set out in your own words your understanding of an idea or situation.

A good statement section will always be fairly general and should not get down to specific details or quotations. Why? Because your statement section signals what the upcoming area of discussion will be. Save your detail and quotations for the evidence section which follows. You have established your *understanding* of a key point with your statement; your *analysis* will come later, with your evidence from the text.

 ## THINGS TO DO AND THINK ABOUT

After setting out in your plan all the material you are going to use, start to group it into various headings or areas. Then create statements which sum up what you want to say about each heading/area. List them one under the other. Do they make a coherent line of argument? If they do, you have a miniature version of the essay you are about to write – and your essay is well begun.

DON'T FORGET

A list of your statements will keep you on task. It will also help you to judge your time appropriately. Don't get bogged down in any single one.

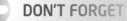 ### DON'T FORGET

A good statement sets out the agenda for the section you are about to embark on. It also announces the general area for discussion. Save the back-up evidence (detailed textual reference and quotations) for the upcoming analysis. If you get into detail too quickly, what are you going to discuss later?

 ### DON'T FORGET

Don't be scared to open a statement section with a question, particularly if it is reminding the examiner that you are respecting the wording of the question. *So, how does all this help our understanding of the text as a whole? Well, for a start ...*

STRUCTURING YOUR PARAGRAPHS

EVIDENCE: BACKING UP YOUR STATEMENTS

By this time, you have gathered together a group of factual statements that form the backbone of your essay. But this is only a skeleton of the full essay: what you need now is *evidence* to back up the facts laid out in your statements. In other words, as in your analysis answers in Close Reading, you need *evidence* from the text to give conviction to what you have just claimed in your statements.

What is evidence?

Evidence takes two forms: direct quotations or detailed references to information from the text. A good essay will make use of both.

Now, since we have already researched relevant quotations for our plan, we can begin to think of providing this as *evidence* – or *analysis* – to back up our statements.

DON'T FORGET

Evidence cannot be plonked into the paragraph; it must be **woven** into your own text.

✗ Wrong: The building was very rundown: *bore in every feature the marks of ... negligence.*

✓ Correct: The building was very rundown, with Stevenson telling us that it *'bore in every feature the marks of ... negligence'.*

DON'T FORGET

Quotations are a very important feature of your essay; treat them with respect by making sure that they *flow* smoothly in and out of your own text. Don't just deposit them into the essay and hope the examiners will be impressed. They won't be.

ONLINE

To find out more about Robert Louis Stevenson and *The Strange Case of Dr Jekyll and Mr Hyde*, go to the Robert Louis Stevenson website at www.brightredbooks.net/ N5English.

ONLINE TEST

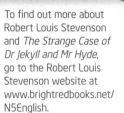

For more practice structuring your paragraphs, test yourself online at www. brightredbooks.net/ N5English.

LET'S TRY THAT OUT

In the opening chapter of *The Strange Case of Dr Jekyll and Mr Hyde*, Stevenson goes to great trouble to establish that the area around Jekyll's laboratory home presents a setting which is a curious mixture of the prosperous and the dingy. We find that *'the street shone out in contrast to its dingy neighbourhood, like a fire in a forest'*; and Stevenson notes the buildings' *'freshly painted shutters, well-polished brasses, and general cleanliness'.*

But yet another contrast awaits us, since Jekyll's laboratory sticks out harshly into this attractive setting: *'a certain sinister block of building thrust forward its gable on the street'.*

Furthermore, we are told that it *'bore in every feature the marks of prolonged and sordid negligence'* and that the door itself was *'blistered and distained. Tramps slouched in the recess ...'*

So, have we backed up our opening statement with enough evidence to support our claim that the area under discussion is a mixture of the shabby and the smart? The answer has to be 'yes': our quotations have established both. We have provided a real *analysis* of the presentation of the area. But is this enough to make a convincing paragraph in an essay of this kind? Can we leave the paragraph just here and move on? Not at all. We need to provide a *commentary* on all this, explaining why we think this is an important point to be making about setting.

COMMENTARY: CLINCHING YOUR CASE

Having looked at evidence, let's explore the next feature of our paragraph: the commentary.

After providing your evidence, you need to go a little further and suggest to the examiner what all this points to. In other words, you need to unpack the evidence a little and show how it establishes the point(s) you made back in your statement. You need, if you like, to *evaluate* its significance for the reader. So, how do you go about this?

The importance of the lead-in phrase

To help your paragraph flow smoothly, you will need a number of lead-in phrases to move the reader from the evidence to your commentary, phrases such as:

From evidence such as this, we can see that ...

Clearly, then, ...

This suggests that ...

From this, we may understand that ...

Alert readers will note that ...

Let's see how such phrases can help you with an explanation and comment on the above section of your paragraph. Continuing from *Tramps slouched in the recess ...,* we might write:

Clearly then, Stevenson is suggesting that the area surrounding Jekyll is far from uniform: a dingy neighbourhood surrounds a smart street, and the smart street has a sinister, squalid building 'thrust' into it. In other words, this is a neighbourhood whose identity is not clear-cut, one where the sordid cannot be separated from the attractive. For the moment, we wonder why Stevenson is making this point quite heavily.

And there your paragraph is complete!

You have made a **Statement** setting out a point about Jekyll's surroundings (showing *understanding* of the text).	S
You have produced **Evidence** to back up this point (showing *analysis* of the means by which you came to this understanding).	E
You have helped the reader with an explanation of what all this evidence is suggesting by providing a **Commentary** on it all (showing an *evaluation* of the evidence's implications).	C

Using the SEC format will help you to keep your paragraphs on track in a way that showcases your knowledge. It also gives the examiner a clear pathway to follow your arguments along.

DON'T FORGET

Statement
SAY IT

Evidence
SHOW IT

Commentary
SELL IT

THINGS TO DO AND THINK ABOUT

The skills that helped you make sense of Close Reading questions – the ability to understand (shown in your **Statement**), analyse (shown in your **Evidence**) and evaluate (shown in your **Commentary**) – are once more proving useful in structuring persuasive critical essays. This is because the body paragraphs are structured around these same ideas which are written in the SEC format described above. The SEC structure is the building block of the body paragraphs of critical essays. Use it.

INTRODUCTIONS AND CONCLUSIONS

Your plan outlines the answer you want to give to the set question. Given your limited time in the exam, you are anxious to get on with it. But be careful. A top essay needs a satisfactory introduction and conclusion to frame the body paragraphs of your essay. So, let's take a look at how we might go about structuring them.

INTRODUCTIONS

A sound introduction suggests to examiners that you are a serious candidate. Here you reassure them that your intentions for answering the question have been intelligently planned and that your knowledge of the text is thorough. Done well, your introduction will give the examiner a favourable impression for marking the rest of the essay. Establish in your mind the following checklist for a successful introduction:

1   In your first sentence, make clear the title of the selected text (in inverted commas!) and its author.

2   In that same sentence, adopt some wording which suggests that you have chosen this text because it fits the set question.

Going back to our earlier 'Jekyll and Hyde' question, you might cover points 1 and 2 by recycling some wording from the question to give:

> A novel in which <u>setting figures prominently</u> is 'The Strange Case of Dr Jekyll and Mr Hyde' by Robert Louis Stevenson.

3   Follow this with a very brief summary – no more than four or five lines – of what happens in the novel.

> Here, respectable Dr Jekyll, impatient with the restraints of respectability, longs to indulge his hidden evil desires. A skilled scientist, he devises a potion to transform himself into Mr Hyde, a wicked character who lives out Jekyll's evil ambitions. But instead of finding lasting release, Jekyll finds he is on the path to ruin.

4   Now revisit the wording of the second part of the question to assure the examiner you have not forgotten about that second part.

> By drawing attention frequently to the physical setting, the time of day and weather, Stevenson uses these features of setting to help us understand what he is saying about the text as a whole.

Note that, in this example, we are giving not just a reference **back** to the question but also a reference **forward** to our 'road-plan' for the essay: discussion of the physical setting to be followed by discussion of times of day and weather (in that order).

Your introduction is your first opportunity to impress the examiner. A sharply focused laying-out of what is to come indicates that you have acquired a mastery of both essay structure and your text. Handled badly, your introduction will signal to the examiner that you have not organised your thoughts sufficiently, and he/she will be wary of the succeeding paragraphs. So, make sure you spend time getting it right.

DON'T FORGET

If you find your plot summary is going on for much more than four or five lines, there is something terribly wrong with it. Stop immediately. Give just enough to make sense of the plot's outline. You need time to construct your case, not to retell the story.

ONLINE TEST

For more practice on introductions, test yourself online at www.brightredbooks.net/N5English.

CONCLUSIONS

Don't let the pressure of time in the exam room put you off attempting a conclusion that rounds off convincingly the arguments you have been putting forward in the previous paragraphs. It doesn't need to be all that long, but it does need to perform certain tasks to clinch your standing as a credible commentator on literature. There are a few guidelines that are worth respecting here.

1   The first sentence of this concluding paragraph should refer back to some wording of the question itself. Here you are reminding the examiner you have kept to the original task.

   Standing back from the text as a whole, we see that setting has been useful in helping to understand it. Stevenson has ...

   Note there is also an opening phrase which signals you are rounding off the essay.

2   You should go on to sum up _briefly_ the main points you have been making in the central section of your essay.

3   On no account bring in new points or quotations at this late stage. It will only spoil the sharp focus of the case you have been making throughout your essay.

Leave time for a conclusion, however short, otherwise your essay will simply stop rather than arrive at a convincing note of finality.

ONLINE

Read the handout 'Conclusions' for more on writing a good conclusion: www.brightredbooks.net/N5English. When you are struggling with what to write, play the 'So what?' game and refocus your mind.

THINGS TO DO AND THINK ABOUT

Test your introduction for efficiency! Ask a partner to read it through and have them try to work out what the original question was. If they can do this, then your introduction is functioning well.

MAINTAINING THE FLOW

Talk to an examiner, and they will tell you that the most successful critical essays follow a clear line of thought from start to finish. Readers should not be pulled abruptly from one topic to another and expected to see a link between them somehow. Skilled candidates should give some serious thought to linking topic to topic, and paragraph to paragraph, and to signalling an upcoming conclusion. There are a number of signalling words, phrases and techniques which will help you achieve this goal.

ONLINE

Discover some of the simpler signalling words by looking at 'Signal Words' from www.brightredbooks.net/N5English. Many of these you already use to change direction, sequence events or illustrate your points. Familiarise yourself with the whole range available to you. Once you have done this, look at how the longer phrases we discuss below can also help you improve the flow of your writing.

DON'T FORGET

By spending time practising writing effective linking statements, you will dramatically improve your writing style and therefore your chance of success in the exam!

DON'T FORGET

Note that all these sentences would make suitable Statements which you could develop successfully to create a convincing SEC paragraph.

FROM INTRODUCTION TO FIRST PARAGRAPH

A sensible idea in your introduction is to indicate in its last lines the areas you will be covering in your essay – creating a 'road-map', if you like. So, your introduction might end with the words:

Donovan arouses sympathy for the protagonist through her handling of Miss O'Halloran's social isolation, the use of **symbolism** *and the second-person narrative.*

Make sure you pick up these three topics (her social isolation, the use of symbolism and the second-person narrative) *in the order mentioned* here, beginning the first SEC paragraph after the introduction with phrases such as:

Examining first Miss O'Halloran's social isolation, we notice that ...

Isolated socially, Miss O'Halloran has only ...

The social isolation of Miss O'Halloran is insisted on by Donovan throughout the short story.

FROM ONE BODY PARAGRAPH TO THE NEXT

Once you have completed your discussion of your first point, your task is to ease the reader from this paragraph to your next point smoothly. In this example, you must lead the reader from your paragraph about Miss O'Halloran's 'social isolation' to your next paragraph, which should discuss the 'symbolism' in the story, the second area you mentioned in your road-map. This can be done effectively by using statements like these:

The sympathy aroused by the old lady's social isolation is further intensified by Donovan's use of symbolism.

Equally effective in arousing our sympathy for Miss O'Halloran is the way Donovan uses symbolism.

Symbolism is the second technique by which Donovan invokes our sympathy for her protagonist.

Successful flow is ensured by making a brief reference – direct or indirect – to the subject of your previous paragraph in the first sentence of your new one.

Once completed, this paragraph needs to be linked to the next one in the way you have done for this one. And so on.

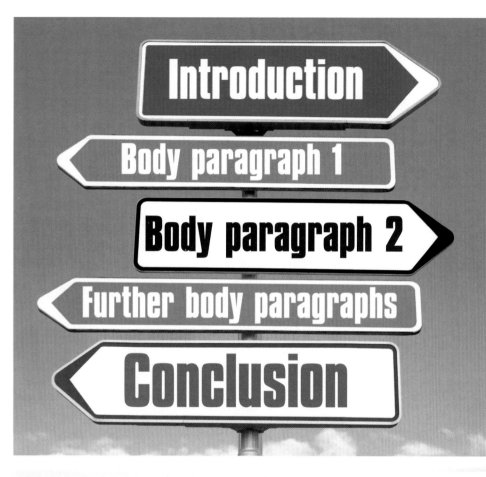

ONLINE

Read this *Guardian* article online: 'A sea of red that evokes thoughts of more than just algae' at www.brightredbooks.net/N5English – can you see how the first statement of each paragraph links to what has come before? This gives it a great flow and makes it easier to read. The same is true in your critical essay-writing.

ONLINE TEST

For more practice on maintaining the flow, test yourself at www.brightredbooks.net/N5English.

DON'T FORGET

Writing a strong introduction is crucial if you want to succeed in your critical essay. However, a smooth flow from paragraph to paragraph is equally important because it helps the reader to understand that there is continuity in your thought – and in your paragraphs.

INDICATING A CONCLUSION

Your essay's flow is neatly rounded off by signalling that the final stages are approaching with a 'summing-up' phrase, followed by a reminder of what was said in the introduction.

Seen overall, this is a short story in which the author successfully employs the techniques of … to bring us close to the misery of …

Standing back, we note that throughout the tale the techniques mentioned in the introduction have succeeded in …

Summing up, we have seen the three techniques of … have been successfully employed to arouse our sympathy for a character who …

Not only is a conclusion indicated by an opening phrase of the type employed here, but also there is a reminder to the examiner of your loyalty to the points you raised in your introduction. In this way, your essay is rounded off in a thoroughly satisfactory manner.

THINGS TO DO AND THINK ABOUT

Before testing out these suggested guidelines to improve the flow of your writing in a brand new essay, why not try this experiment? This you might do with a partner.

Take an essay which you have already written, and adapt the techniques and phrases we have been suggesting here to assist the smooth flow from one paragraph to the next. Do it in such a way that you lead smoothly from introduction to first paragraph, from paragraph to paragraph and then into the conclusion. You do not need to rewrite the whole essay, just the necessary linking sentences. Now read these links aloud to a partner. You will notice that you have added real authority to your writing. Try it.

PERFECTING YOUR PERFORMANCE

You are now in a position to create a successful critical essay. But there is always room to polish your performance to ensure optimum marks. Let's see how.

USING QUOTATIONS FOR MAXIMUM EFFECT

Longer quotations

There is more than one way to introduce a long quotation to your paragraph.

Sometimes you will pave the way for a quotation by first describing it. In this case, you should use a colon (:), drop a line, indent slightly and begin the quotation using inverted commas. This gives us:

Her clear-sighted sadness is seen in the words:

> *'I have betrayed a great man, and his like will never be seen again.'*

Sometimes your sentence will not describe the quotation but simply introduce it. In this case, the colon would only interrupt the natural flow of the words. So, instead, you should write:

Her clear-sighted sadness is seen when she comments that she has

> *'betrayed a great man, and his like will never be seen again'.*

Always make sure your longer quotations have room to breathe; drop a line (with or without a colon), indent slightly and add quotation marks. Drop another line before continuing your own text.

Shorter quotations

A good essay will have a mixture of longer and shorter quotations. Shorter ones can be just as effective as longer ones. If the longer quotation escapes you in full, you can use the remembered parts to great effect.

For instance, if you wanted to use the quotation

'the street shone out in contrast to its dingy neighbourhood, like a fire in a forest'

but you could not quite remember it in full, you could use the remembered phrases to good effect and paraphrase the rest.

The street is described as making a sharp contrast to its 'dingy neighbourhood' and standing out 'like a fire in a forest'.

As long as you weave the short quotations seamlessly into your own text, this kind of paraphrase-plus-quotation will prove more effective than a longer, misquoted extract. It may also pinpoint more sharply the exact point you wish to make.

GIVING A CONTEXT

There is a danger of assuming that readers understand more than they do. No quotation, however well chosen, will make its desired effect unless you give it a brief *context*. In other words, indicate briefly not just who said it but also why and under what circumstances it was said. If, for instance, you had been reading *Macbeth* and wanted to comment about King Duncan's generosity of nature, you might want to mention his kindness to a wounded messenger – but be careful how you do it.

contd

DON'T FORGET

If you can't remember the exact wording of the extract you wish to quote in your essay, a series of short quotes will serve you just as well – if not better!

ONLINE

For a more detailed review of how to use quotations correctly in your essay, read 'The Writer's Handbook: Using literary quotations' at www.brightredbooks.net/N5English.

Duncan shows he has a great generosity of nature:

   'Go get him surgeons.'

Duncan has a great generosity of nature. Seeing a badly wounded messenger collapse, he personally orders him to be taken care of:

   'Go get him surgeons.' ✔

A context does not need to be long; it simply needs to lead readers into the quotation in a way that helps them to make sense of the point you are making.

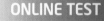

ONLINE TEST

For more practice on perfecting your performance, test yourself online at www.brightredbooks.net/N5English.

MAKING YOUR LEAD-IN WORK FOR YOU

Make sure your lead-in to the quotation does not simply repeat the content of the quotation. For example, in this description about *Buddha Da* by Anne Donovan, a bad lead-in would be:

Jimmy tells his wife he is going on a journey but he is not sure where he is going:

   'Ah'm on a journey but ah don't know where ah'm gaun.'

The lead-in here might better be:

Jimmy comes across to his wife – and to readers – as rather vague about his plans for taking his study of Buddhism forward:

   'Ah'm on a journey but ah don't know where ah'm gaun.'

In other words, a thoughtful lead-in does more than simply help the reader to understand the quotation's context; it can also underline your ability to evaluate its significance.

THINGS TO DO AND THINK ABOUT

It is difficult to identify exactly the moment when an examiner decides to award a top grade. There is an accumulation of factors at work here. These are some of the key ones which should be studied well in advance of entering the exam room.

- You need to demonstrate a thorough knowledge of your texts. That means reading them not just in class but regularly on your own as well.

- You must select *only* the information from your text knowledge which answers the specific question in front of you. Examiners do not want to know everything your teacher has taught you.

- You must be alert to all sections of the question and apportion your time accordingly.

- You need a plan to help you structure a coherent essay which is more than a loose collection of good points. There should be a line of argument that the examiner can follow easily as one paragraph flows smoothly into the next.

- Each paragraph should be carefully structured to ensure that your claims are borne out by evidence and that you unpack this evidence for the reader. In other words, you make a **S**tatement, back it up with **E**vidence and then give a **C**ommentary on it before moving on to the next paragraph (**SEC**).

- A soundly structured introduction will help you to stay on task, and a 'road-map' in the introduction's last sentence will help examiners to find their way round your arguments. A brief conclusion reminds them of your key points.

- Use the correct procedure for laying out quotations, long or short. This shows good academic manners and attention to detail that increases your stature as a competent commentator on your texts.

- Make sure that your quotations make sense. This means checking that you have given each one a context, however brief.

TRIAL ESSAY

Now that we've looked at all the bits and pieces that make up a critical essay, let's see what it looks like when we put it all together. Read through the essay, noting the various 'landmarks', and see if you can model your next critical essay on similar lines.

Choose a short story or novel in which setting figures prominently.

Describe the contribution of the setting and then show how this feature helped your understanding of the text as a whole.

Note how underlined phrases pick up wording from the question.	A novel in which <u>setting figures prominently</u> is *The Strange Case of Dr Jekyll and Mr Hyde* by Robert Louis Stevenson. Here, respectable Dr Jekyll, impatient with the restraints of respectability, longs to indulge his hidden evil desires. A skilled scientist, he devises a potion to transform himself into Mr Hyde, a wicked character who lives out Jekyll's evil ambitions. But, instead of finding lasting release, Jekyll finds he is on the path to ruin. By drawing attention frequently to the <u>physical setting</u>, the <u>time of day and weather</u>, Stevenson uses these features of setting to <u>help us understand</u> what he is saying about <u>the text as a whole</u>.
Note how end of introduction emphasises both engagement with the second part of question and lists how the setting is to be handled. A road-map, if you like.	

In the opening chapter, Stevenson signals that the area around Hyde's laboratory home is a mixture of the prosperous and the dingy.

He tells us that

> 'the street shone out in contrast to its dingy neighbourhood, like a fire in a forest.'

and Stevenson notes its '*freshly painted shutters, well-polished brasses, and general cleanliness and gaiety of note.*'

But Hyde's laboratory spoils this attractive setting, for

> '*a certain sinister block of building thrust forward its gable on the street.*'

which

> '*bore in every feature the marks of prolonged and sordid negligence.*'

The doorway itself was

> '*blistered and distained. Tramps slouched in the recess …*'

Statement for SEC1	
Start of Evidence for SEC1	
Start of Commentary for SEC1	Clearly then, Stevenson is suggesting that the area surrounding Jekyll is far from uniform: a dingy neighbourhood surrounds a smart street, and the smart street has a sinister, squalid building 'thrust' into it. In other words, this is a neighbourhood whose identity is not clear-cut, one where the sordid cannot be separated from the attractive. For the moment, we wonder why Stevenson is making this point quite heavily.

Statement for SEC2	Soon there is yet a further contrast of environments, for we learn that this squalid laboratory building is connected to buildings in a nearby square. Why again has Stevenson linked them? We learn that
Start of Evidence for SEC2	

> '*Round the corner from the by street there was a square of ancient, handsome houses, now for the most part decayed from their high estate.*'

This decayed environment, however, is brightened by

> '*One house [which] wore a great air of wealth and comfort …*'

contd

This is the rather splendid home of Dr Jekyll. Stevenson is making the point that there is a duality of identity in these very closely related environments: grubbiness rubs shoulders with smartness. This use of physical setting is key to our understanding of Stevenson's intentions here, for in this novella he is exploring Jekyll's claim that

> '… man is not truly one, but truly two.'

Jekyll believes that man has two sides to his nature: the decent, God-fearing, respectable side which his day-time life as Dr Jekyll represents; and the other, more sordid side of human nature, is the side drawn to the evil and corruption in which his night-time persona, Hyde, revels. Just as sharply contrasting environments can exist side by side in towns and streets, so too can contrasting sides of human nature coexist in the same being. Jekyll is not unique, it is being discreetly suggested; duality exists all around us, not just in human personalities but in physical environments also.

The setting is further enriched by having key moments in the story take place either at night or at twilight. Enfield's first encounter with Hyde takes place in darkness at:

> 'about three o'clock of a black winter morning.'

The narrator, Utterson, only makes contact with Hyde at night; and one of Hyde's most vicious crimes, the murder of the MP Danvers Carew, also takes place at night. In a tale which explores the darker side of human nature, this insistence on the darkness of night is hardly surprising. It sets up a sombre atmosphere around the many dark events which the story relates. Darkness is the appropriate element in which to set in motion murky, evil deeds.

Weather, <u>too</u>, backs up the mood of the piece in key incidents. Going off in search of Hyde's abode, Utterson comments on the fog, which seemed like

> 'A great-coloured pall [that] lowered over heaven …'

and later that

> '… the fog settled down again upon that part, as brown as umber and cut him off from his blackguardly surroundings.'

Finding an ailing Jekyll in Hyde's laboratory, Utterson notes that, even in the building itself,

> 'the fog began to lie thickly'.

References to fog are further dotted throughout the tale. Like night, fog is an appropriate backdrop to a story exploring the hidden side of human nature. For just as fog gets in the way of seeing clearly, so, too, does Jekyll's behaviour throw an impenetrable cloak around what he is actually doing with his life. Even his closest friends cannot see through this barrier he has thrown up around himself. Fog, therefore, seems a fitting feature of setting with which to surround the narrative.

Standing back from the text as a whole, we see that setting has been useful in helping understand it. Stevenson has used contrasting townscapes to suggest the difficulty of separating the attractive and the murkier aspects of existence. Furthermore, he has underlined this by physically connecting Hyde's laboratory to the grand home of Jekyll. As this is a tale which explores the darker side of human nature, it is only appropriate that night and fog play their part in setting up an atmosphere that is both dark and confusing. Setting, <u>therefore,</u> has <u>helped the reader to understand</u> in graphic, physical terms Stevenson's complex view of the nature of man.

Sidebar annotations:

- Start of Commentary for SEC2
- Statement for SEC3
- Start of Evidence for SEC3
- Start of Commentary for SEC3
- Statement for SEC4
- Start of Evidence for SEC4
- Start of Commentary for SEC4
- Linking phrase to indicate start of conclusion
- The underlined phrases act as a reminder to the examiner that you have fulfilled the task set out in the initial question.

SCOTTISH LITERATURE IN NATIONAL 5

If you want to see your country hale and whole
Turn back the pages of fourteen hundred years.

(Edwin Morgan, 'Retrieving and Renewing')

National 5 sees the welcome return of the study of Scottish literature to its rightful place in the curriculum of Scottish schools. And, while the texts you will be studying may not extend back 1400 years, they will do much to help you discover the riches that we in Scotland enjoy from our writers past and present. These are riches for us to relish as readers and to inspire us as writers.

ONLINE

For a rich source of background information on Scottish literature, check out the Association for Scottish Literary Studies via www. brightredbooks.net/N5English

WHY WE SHOULD STUDY SCOTTISH LITERATURE?

Someone who has played his part in helping Scottish literature to resume its rightful place in the literary curriculum is Alan Riach, Professor of Scottish Literature at Glasgow University. Here, he reminds us how Scottish literature amply rewards its study.

Dear Student,

Continuing discoveries, and a healthy appetite for them, is what it's all about: enjoying the company of poems, songs, plays and stories, finding out about other people, places, taking the voyage out and finding your way home. Edwin Morgan described writing a poem – or reading a poem – as being like going on a journey in a spaceship, into unknown constellations, unmapped territory, uncharted seas, to discover things that will help you in the future, where no predictions are certain. All the Scottish writers you will meet in your reading at school should do this.

The most essential element of Scotland is its variety, and Scottish literature is various in time and place, language and tone, ways of understanding the world and attitudes towards our experience of it, the ways and wiles of others. Sometimes Scottish literature, like the country itself, delivers things that are truly profound, deeply necessary and refreshing. Sometimes the shock of new perception is followed by the warmth of recognition. It has to be fun to read it and teach it, and always has been for me. The pleasure it gives illuminates and opens questions, asks us to consider things from points of view we might not have thought of before, and in forms of language so diverse they may seem very unfamiliar and strange. That is the virtue of its invitation: try the words out, in your own voice. See how they apply, what they mean, what they sound like when you bring them from your throat, what they look like when you study them on the page.

We always need this, to get through life: to make some kind of sense from the chaos of the world. The quest is to take us beyond ourselves, to find something else – something we're not, but perhaps something we are related to, something that connects.

This is what all literature does. Every single poem, song, play, story, novel gives us a way of looking at the world. It embodies an attitude to experience. It takes us to other places, to meet other people, to understand other ways of life,

contd

politics, religions, women and men, children and old folks, animals, geology, landscapes, economies and ways of seeing how things work. Everything is open to our enquiry: not only the good and the bad, but the ugly as well.

We begin from where we are, in whatever part of Scotland we find ourselves, city or village, island archipelago or farmland or small town, to ask questions. Who has written about this place? What languages did they use? When did they write and how have things changed here, since then? What are the good things around us? What are the bad things that need to be changed?

This is what literature helps us to do.

It has to be a pleasure in itself, but it also opens up the world to all of us, anyone who cares enough to read deeply. For you have to care about something to read it deeply. As Herman Melville says, 'Any fish can swim near the surface, but it takes a great whale to go down stairs five miles or more'. Or as Hugh MacDiarmid puts it in Scots:

Like staundin' water in a pocket o'   *Like standing water in a pocket of*
Impervious clay I pray I'll never be,   *Impervious clay I pray I'll never be,*
Cut-aff and self-sufficient, but let reenge   *Cut-off and self-sufficient, but let range*

Heichts o' the lift and benmaist deeps o' sea.   *Heights of the sky and furthest depths of sea.*

One last thing. If you like a poem, song or story, memorise it. Actors learn their lines. We all have stories to tell. Learning a poem by heart can help get words into your mind most deeply, and the words themselves help sharpen your perception. They keep thinking clear and senses keen. Flowers and fruit have better colour and taste when you put them in words. Identify trees, cloud forms, structures of economy, specific aspects of people, in words, and you start to understand them more precisely and more deeply. And one more last thing: don't be shy of saying what you think. All art, literature especially, is a living conversation. My best advice: speak about these things to other people.

Professor Alan Riach
University of Glasgow

ONLINE

Check out the multiple facets of Scottish literature. Go to '100 Best Scottish Books' at www.brightredpublishing.net/N5English

 THINGS TO DO AND THINK ABOUT

Think about Alan Riach's last thought: 'don't be shy of saying what you think. All art, literature especially, is a living conversation. My best advice: speak about these things to other people.' National 5 offers you a real chance to keep that 'living conversation' going. Make the most of it as you talk and listen throughout the various activities of the course.

USING ACQUIRED KNOWLEDGE PROFITABLY

What you probably will have noticed so far about your National 5 course is that the skills that you have acquired in one area of study bring you substantial benefits in another. Happily, the Critical Reading section in which you explore Scottish texts is no different. Here again our old friends understanding, analysis and evaluation reappear.

RECAP: SKILLS LEARNED

So, let's just remind ourselves how some of the skills that you learned for Close Reading work will serve you well again as you analyse these Scottish texts.

- **Summarising.** You should be prepared to summarise sections of the extract in question. Before you start, look back to refresh your memory on how to do this. See page 50.

- **Figurative language.** Here, more than ever, your knowledge of metaphors, similes, personification, alliteration, onomatopoeia and all the other devices you already know about will help you to detect how the writer's language is making its effect on readers. And remember, it is the *effect* of the device that matters most, not just the ability to spot it. See page 32.

- **Word choice.** Along with the features of **sentence structure** you know about, word choice will also help you to gauge how authors set about influencing their readers with the choice of one word or structure rather than another. See page 36.

- **Tone.** What you have already learned about tone will be of service here again in searching out the tone or mood that writers are attempting to convey to you. See page 44.

Our list could go on for some time. In short, there is very little knowledge which you have already acquired here that will not prove useful. Now is the time to revisit the Close Reading section and to familiarise yourself with the glossary of critical terms and literary devices on page 127.

LOOKING FOR LINKS

Now, while much of what you are being asked to do here is quite familiar to you, there are aspects of the course which break new ground. National 5 requires you to get to know a number of prose, drama and poetry texts from the rich heritage of Scottish literature in real depth. This means that the reading skills we have outlined above, while remaining crucial to success in your understanding, analysis and evaluation of the passage, are not the end of the story.

You will also need to *know* the studied text(s) in considerable detail. Why? Well, in addition to explaining how writers create certain effects, you will also need to be able to point to links or connections between groups of poems or groups of short stories by the selected author – or, in the case of prose or drama, how the novelist or playwright explores elsewhere in the work ideas touched on here in the extract under study. The question which asks you to make these connections is a high-value one, usually accounting for 8 of the 20 marks on offer. So, it needs to be approached seriously. How do we go about looking for these links in each of the genres? Let's see.

Poetry

You will be asked to study six poems from the works of your selected poet. Only one poem will feature in the extract offered for analysis. The final question, however, will invite you

contd

DON'T FORGET

When a question mentions the writer's 'language', you are in luck. For here you can point to a whole range of techniques including imagery, sentence structure, punctuation, tone and word choice.

ONLINE

Stay up to date with the latest in Scottish poetry by following 'Scottish Poetry Library' on Twitter: www.brightredbooks.net/ N5English.

to make connections between ideas and/or language you have noticed here and in the other five poems by the same poet.

In terms of ideas, perhaps we see the poet returning in several poems to portray characters who parallel or contrast with others in, say, their ways of thinking, reacting or relating to others. Perhaps there are situations in relationships which crop up more than once. In terms of language, perhaps we see a fondness for, say, a conversational tone with enjambment as a recurring feature of style. Is the poem rich in other poetic devices, or is it deliberately matter-of-fact, using everyday language? Does the poet appear in the poem, or is there some other speaker narrating the poem? Are some poems written in free verse, or has the poet used a specific form? In Scots or English? You need always to be alert to making connections at several possible levels between the ideas and language of the offered poem and at least one other poem you have studied.

Prose

If you have chosen to study one of the selections of short stories, there will be some overlap between your approach to them and what we have been saying about poetry above. Check if there are certain ideas or situations in the extract which link it to at least one of the five other stories of your choice: lack of communication between the generations, for example. Or scenes in which characters confront or misunderstand each other, perhaps?

If you have chosen to study a novel, the situation is slightly different. Here you are looking for other incidents in the novel where you can spot, say, a character reacting in a way similar to or perhaps contrasting with previous behaviour, or in a manner which shows developing understanding or emotional depth. What has happened in between times to bring about this change? Perhaps one character is viewed in several ways by others in the novel? Maybe a theme is revisited in a way which parallels or contrasts with its treatment elsewhere in the novel? Are there other scenes where setting or atmosphere seems particularly important? What does setting contribute to the overall effect of the incident on the reader? Has setting been used this way before?

Drama

Many of the points about character, theme and setting discussed above with regard to poetry and prose also hold good for a context passage taken from a play. With the play, however, the action unrolls via dialogue, which needs to be carefully examined for typical speech characteristics. Do some characters have topics to which they regularly return? Do characters typically appear asking questions, giving instructions, sounding optimistic or pessimistic, talking about trivia, being violent, needing help, saying little or too much? How well do characters listen to each other? Are there moments when this changes? What is the effect on us of the change? Are there stage props which take on symbolic meanings in different parts of the play? Does lighting change at any key points? And what is the effect of this? Do the costumes of the characters change at any point? What do the changes tell us?

 THINGS TO DO AND THINK ABOUT

By drawing on reading skills that you already possess, and developing new ones to look for links and connections within plays and novels; between poems and short stories, you are getting to the heart of what Critical Reading is all about – and to the heart of the author's creative processes.

ONLINE TEST

Take the 'Using acquired knowledge profitably' test online at www. brightredbooks.net/ N5English.

RONA MUNRO, *BOLD GIRLS*: AN INTRODUCTION

Born in Aberdeen in 1959, the daughter of a radiotherapist and a Geology lecturer, Rona Munro was fascinated by playwriting from an early age. After studying at Edinburgh University, she quickly established herself as a rising star in drama circles with commissions for plays, screenplays and radio plays. Written in 1991, *Bold Girls* won Munro the 1991 London Critics Circle Theatre Award for Most Promising New Playwright. It deals with the everyday lives of four women whose menfolk have been either killed or imprisoned for their roles in the 'troubles' in Northern Ireland.

OUTLINE

The action takes place in the course of a late afternoon, evening and early morning in the West Belfast of what Munro, writing in 1991, calls 'today'. Three neighbours, Marie, Nora and Cassie, have their already difficult lives disrupted by the arrival of the mysterious young girl, Deirdre. Despite presenting the appearance of mutually supportive closeness, the trio pursue various consoling dreams which underline their isolation and which camouflage underlying tensions. Deirdre, in her search for the truth about her father, serves as a catalyst to revealing these cracks. Despite its many humorous moments, the play's searing examination of the stereotypical roles of men and women in the material-driven society of today gives it a significance which transcends Northern Irish boundaries.

DON'T FORGET

The page references in this section are from Hodder Gibson's 1995 edition of *Bold Girls*!

CHARACTERS

Marie

'Cheerful, efficient, young' widow of Michael, whose image looks out on the living room. She overtly avoids any thought of a stain on his memory but is increasingly disturbed by the young girl in white who has begun to haunt her house as she tries to bring up her sons Mickey and Brendan to respect their father's memory.

Cassie

Long-term friend of Marie is the 'sceptical, sharp-tongued' daughter of Nora, with whom she enjoys an uneasy relationship due to their conflicting views on Nora's dead husband and Cassie's father, Sean. The truth about Sean – violent brute of a husband or a man provoked beyond endurance by nagging – remains elusive throughout the play. She dreams of fleeing Belfast to start a new life, free from the drabness of provincial life and the guilt of knowing she had an affair with Marie's husband, Michael. This is a secret which emerges late in the play, partly due to the arrival of Deirdre.

Nora

Source of much of the play's humour, Nora protects herself from the pain of a failed marriage, her judgemental daughter and the daily trials of living in violence-torn Belfast by retreating largely into a world of interior decoration.

Deirdre

Emerges out of the 'darkness' of the violence around her, seeking the truth about her father, probably Michael, and the chance to come in from the cold, possibly by finding a home with Marie. Nurtured in violence, she has no qualms initially about revenging herself on society by stealing and destroying whatever comes to hand. The play ends in the hope of a new life for her with Marie.

THEMES

According to Professor Douglas Gifford,

> '*Munro's main theme is a satire on the way ordinary people live now – not just in Northern Ireland, but in the west, and indeed in any culture which imbalances the sexes in their social roles, encouraging stereotyping of male dominance and social privilege and female subservience to that behaviour.*'

This we see in the way the men – who never appear – are pandered to by the women, even though from what we hear of their gambling, drinking, fighting and promiscuity, they are hardly worthy recipients of this attention.

There is, however, another major theme which helps inform the action of the play. In Scene 2, Deirdre comments:

> '*The whole town's a prison, smash chunks off the walls 'cause we're all in a prison.*'

When we examine the lives of the three women, we see that Deirdre is not far from the truth. While a number of their men are certainly in Long Kesh prison, the women, too, are similarly confined, not simply in a society that privileges men, but in one where their lives are caught in a web of television game shows, films and soap operas and the cheapening materialism of peach-coloured polyester, Mickey's raspberry ice-cream syrup, magi-mixes and Black-and-Decker drills – the world of contemporary western culture, Munro seems to suggest.

But, it could be argued, this materialism is as much refuge as prison for these women as they struggle with the difficulties of reconciling their lives with a version of the truth with which they can live – one of the play's several sub-themes, which we will explore on the next page.

THINGS TO DO AND THINK ABOUT

Why do you think Munro chose to write the play from the perspective of the women left behind, rather than the people caught up in the violence itself?

DON'T FORGET

When analysing drama, remember a play is not simply words on a page; it is a living thing, a performance in which ideas and themes come alive not simply through the characters' dialogue but also through the contribution of setting, clothes, music, lighting, props and stage effects. Keep this in mind when discussing the play. This is a play rich in hints from its stagecraft. Deirdre's knife and Michael's picture are just two. Think of others.

ONLINE

Read Douglas Gifford's full article, 'Making them bold and breaking the mould', at www.brightredbooks.net/ N5English

ONLINE TEST

Take the '*Bold Girls*: An Introduction' test online at www.brightredbooks.net/ N5English

RONA MUNRO, *BOLD GIRLS*: SUB-THEMES

ATTITUDES TO THE TRUTH

Truth is always an elusive commodity – and nowhere more so than in this play. What *is* the truth behind Sean's violence towards Nora: a violent drunk or a good man provoked beyond endurance? And what are we to think of Joe, Cassie's husband? To Nora, he is a sound provider; to Cassie, a drunken oaf. To what extent exactly did Marie suspect her Michael of carrying on with other women? This difficulty in negotiating the truth drives the women into different positions.

Marie, whatever her suspicions, studiously *avoids confronting the truth*, telling her sons that

> *Your daddy was a good man and a brave man and he did the best he could and he's in heaven watching out for you and that's what [...] keeps me going, keeps me strong ...*

This mental image – and the physical image of Michael on the wall – comforts and sustains her as she goes about her life.

Cassie has spent some effort in *concealing the truth* about her relationship with Michael from Marie, which adds to her desire to escape what she sees as the grim, restricting provincial life of West Belfast.

Nora *flees the truth* of her bleak existence – her husband dead, a son in prison and herself the victim of military and domestic violence – by seeking comfort in maintaining and decorating her home, a trim retreat from reality. With a new roll of cut-price peach-coloured polyester, she is convinced 'That'll be my front room just a wee dream again.'

Deirdre is the only one of the quartet who is actively *seeking the truth*: the truth about her paternity, a truth that will give her a home with Marie, she hopes, and allow her into a family life of the kind she has heretofore been deprived of, thereby escaping from the circle of violence and theft which seems to have been her life so far.

TALKING WITHOUT COMMUNICATING

There is no shortage of chat and banter in the play. Indeed, its robust interchanges are at the heart of the play's appeal. But there are various points in the play when we hear Marie, Cassie and Nora talking completely at cross-purposes, with no-one really listening to anyone else. The effect can at times be humorous, as in the play's opening lines. But, at others, it emphasises the essential distance that exists between the women.

Despite a surface appearance of closeness and solidarity, they are essentially three lonely women who often fail in daily life to communicate to one another their doubts and fears. When they do, as happens in Scene 4, the results are disastrous, although it leads finally to a clearing of the air. This stifling of real communication is a sad but very necessary means of papering over the underlying cracks in the relationship between Marie and Cassie, and between Cassie and her mother. These recurring 'cross-talks' are one of Munro's ways of signalling their essential isolation in what appears to be a mutually supportive quasi-family.

DON'T FORGET

Watching carefully how characters interact – or do not interact – with each other is vital to understanding the inner lives of these women.

Photo from the 1994 production of 'Bold Girls', at The Matrix Theatre, Los Angeles.

THE CONSOLING DREAM

To sustain them in their lives, the four women have forged their own consoling dreams. For Cassie, it is, Marie suggests, a dream of escape to Spain with a toyboy, hence her preoccupation with diets, her appearance in a bikini and the £200 she has stolen from Nora. Nora's dream, as we have seen, concerns escape into a world of peach-coloured polyester. Marie's dream is less materialistic, anchored as it is in a vision of Michael's essential goodness as she goes about tending to her family and feeding the birds. Deirdre, like Marie, is less materialistic in her dream, seeking a refuge from the streets into a family life of which she feels herself deprived. It is her 'wee bit of hard truth' which helps puncture the dreams of the other three; but there is, in the play's final pages, a hint that Marie and Deirdre may find consolation together, a consolation based on a reality stripped of distracting illusions.

THINGS TO DO AND THINK ABOUT

Do you feel that the women have been diminished or trivialised by a society obsessed by materialism (peach-coloured polyester, raspberry ice-cream syrup, *The Price is Right* etc.), or does materialism offer them a welcome relief from an unpleasant reality? Organise a group discussion, making sure you have plenty of textual evidence to back up your viewpoint. This might form a useful outcome for assessment.

ONLINE

For more insight into the setting of *Bold Girls*, read 'A Brief History of Belfast' at www.brightredbooks.net/ N5English.

ONLINE TEST

Take the '*Bold Girls*: Sub-Themes' test online at www.brightredbooks.net/ N5English.

RONA MUNRO, *BOLD GIRLS*: GETTING TO GRIPS WITH THE TEXT

The brief notes you've read in the previous pages will help you to understand the general outline and concerns of the play. In this exercise, however, you need to be able to recognise these concerns in detail.

DON'T FORGET

Note that, in plays, the stage directions need to be taken as seriously as the dialogue itself.

ANALYSING THE PLAY

So, let's take a look both at an extract from Scene Two and at the kind of questions you will need to be prepared for.

Scene Two

The Club

This could be a community hall or even an ancient warehouse, but it has been jazzed up with glitterballs and spots. The chairs and tables are cheap and battered. There are double doors at the back of the room. Marie, Nora and Cassie have got themselves a table overlooking the small dance floor. There is a small stand, like a lectern, on one side of it. The place is crowded, bright with the colours of the women's dresses and great misty clouds of cigarette smoke whirling in the fans. Cassie's dress is quite revealing though not extravagantly so. It is silent. The three women are standing by their chairs, heads bowed as if by a graveside. No one moves, they speak in whispers.

MARIE I didn't know him.

CASSIE There's that cramp again, in my leg. I'll wobble.

NORA That's his aunty there, is it not? She shouldn't be here drinking sure she shouldn't.

MARIE Can't put a face to him at all.

CASSIE My shoes, a size too small and I've swelled with the heat. Oh God, don't let me fall off them.

NORA His mother's sister-in-law's sister, it's close enough. She should be with that poor woman.

MARIE Was he young?

CASSIE Just a boy too.

NORA Is that not a minute over?

MARIE Is that not a minute now?

CASSIE Can I get off my feet?

There is a sudden burst of music and a loud buzz of talk. The women shout over this as they claim their seats with jackets and handbags.

MARIE Did you get my ticket for the competition, Cassie?

CASSIE I got us all ten.

NORA Ten?

MARIE Money to burn.

CASSIE I'm feeling lucky.

MARIE So it's a gin and lime and a Black Russian for you, Nora?

NORA No, I'll get these.

CASSIE Sure I'll get them.

MARIE *(waving a fiver at the waitress)* No you're all right. I've my money in my hand.

CASSIE Let's have a kitty then, fiver in and start us with doubles, Marie.

MARIE I can't catch her eye.

NORA Did you know him then, the poor wee boy?

CASSIE It was him with the dog.

contd

NORA	At the chemist's?
CASSIE	His brother.
MARIE	Always seems such a long minute.
NORA	I was just in that chemist's today.
MARIE	I hate it. Never know what to fill my head with.
NORA	They still hadn't got my prescription in.
MARIE	I didn't know him. What can you fill your head with if you can't picture his face?
CASSIE	You'd know him if you saw him. Just nineteen, trying to grow a moustache like dust on a ledge.
NORA	His mother's youngest. The last one at home.
MARIE	*(shivering)* I still can't see him. I just think of coffins.
NORA	She's all on her own now. All on her own.
CASSIE	Marie, will you hurry up getting that drink, it's the only nourishment I've got coming to me today. This is going to be the wildest of nights. I'm telling you, Mummy, all the times I've been here, the best ones have always been when we've come on our own, just the three of us.

Marie waves her money for the waitress again.

Marie exits.

NORA	Remember the first we knew of what happened to Michael was when they asked us to stand for him?
CASSIE	Marie had never been out of her house, never told a soul till we came in to her.
NORA	Oh, but he was well respected.
CASSIE	Just sitting by the fire and the fire dead for hours and the baby crying and crying …
NORA	They sang for him as well, do you remember?
CASSIE	Her just sitting there.
NORA	He's still missed; there's some men you don't forget.
CASSIE	He was popular, I'll say that for him.
NORA	He was.

QUESTIONS

1   In your own words, summarise what this extract tells us about life in West Belfast for these three women. You should make at least four key points.   4

2   With close reference to the text, show how Marie's reactions in the minute's silence differ from those of Cassie.   2

3   Show how any two examples of Nora's use of language contribute to relieving the grim atmosphere of the boy's death.   2

4   By referring closely to the text, show how the memories of Nora and Cassie differ in their reaction to the death of Michael, and say what this implies about their sympathies at the time.   4

5   Look carefully at the reactions of the women during the minute's silence. Refer to two other moments in the play where the writer uses this same technique for handling dialogue, and say how effective you find it in exploring the theme of isolation.   8

20 marks total

ONLINE

Have a look at the 'National Library of Scotland's Description of *Bold Girls*' at www.brightredbooks.net/ N5English

ONLINE TEST

Take the '*Bold Girls*: Getting to grips with the text' test online at www. brightredbooks.net/N5English

THINGS TO DO AND THINK ABOUT

Try out the questions above, then look at the hints on the next page and see how well you got on.

RONA MUNRO, *BOLD GIRLS*: SOME WAYS OF ANSWERING

How did you get on? Here are some pointers to possible answers and how to find them.

QUESTION 1: HINTS FOR AN ANSWER

We learn quite a lot about the personalities and relationships of Marie, Cassie and Nora throughout the extract, but the question asks us specifically about 'life in West Belfast for these three women'. That means we need to look beyond their relationships in the home and search for signs of what life is like for them in West Belfast during 'the troubles' of the last decades of the twentieth century.

We need four key comments which can be made in bullet-point form. These need to be based on direct evidence from the text and cannot be vague generalisations. Here in italics are some items of textual evidence which will help to steer you to your four key points.

Textual evidence	Key point to be made
1 *the best ones [evenings] have always been when we've come on our own.*	Despite the 'troubles', they still go out to a club to enjoy themselves. (1) Their successful evenings are not dependent on their menfolk. (1)
2 *chairs and tables are cheap and battered*	They frequent places which are not particularly chic or classy. (1)
3 *'standing by their chairs, heads bowed as if by a grave-side'/ they asked us to stand for him*	Death is no stranger to their social lives. ('Standing' being a mark of respect to the dead – mentioned twice in extract). (1)
4 *It was him with the dog/that's his aunty there*	The women live in a close-knit community where relationships are known. (1)
5 *So it's a gin and lime and a Black Russian for you, Nora?*	They are ready to spend money on enjoying themselves (although money seems to be not plentiful). (1)

QUESTION 2: HINTS TO AN ANSWER

Here you need to pick out words or expressions (of the kind we selected in Question 1) which show how Marie and Cassie are different in the way they behave and think during the minute's silence, and then say what these remarks reveal. You will get marks for one quotation and a detailed comment, or for two quotations with more straightforward comments.

So, you might select:

Didn't know him/can't put a face to him/Was he young?

These comments suggest that the dead young man is very much at the forefront of Marie's thoughts, even if she did not know this particular victim personally. (1)

There's that cramp again, in my leg/My shoes, a size too small/don't let me fall off them.

Cassie's remarks suggest that her own personal comfort blots out any thought of the dead young man. Marie is thinking of others; Cassie is thinking of herself. (1)

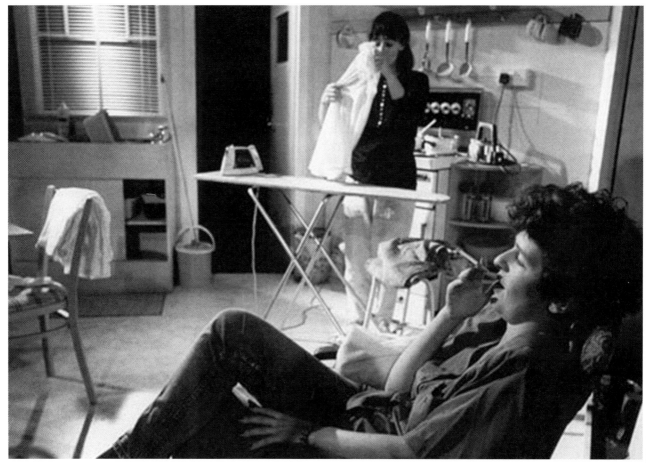

Photo from the original 1991 production of 'Bold Girls', at Cumbernauld Theatre.

QUESTION 3: HINTS TO AN ANSWER

When asked to find 'two examples of Nora's use of language', you need look through Nora's comments for two which may be a little odd/out of place/funny at what should be a rather solemn moment marking the brutal death of a young boy. How do they 'relieve' the 'grim atmosphere'?

His mother's sister-in-law's sister; it's close enough.

At a time of mourning, her exaggerated concern with placing exactly a woman's distant relationship to the dead boy seems humorously out of place, making the audience smile. (1)

They still hadn't got my prescription in.

The dead boy's connection with the chemist's reminds her of a personal irritation with the shop. Again, this seems oddly humorous, given the solemnity of the occasion. (1)

THINGS TO DO AND THINK ABOUT

So, how are you getting on? These first questions are excellent practice in developing some of the typical skills needed for this section of the paper:

(a) summarising with close reference the text to make points in your own words

(b) selecting precise evidence to suggest what exact point Munro is making by its inclusion

Were you maybe generalising too much? In their different ways, each question is asking you for an answer in direct response to the text in front of you. Compare answers with people around you to see how you all got on. Practice will see you learning to familiarise yourself with the precision required.

ONLINE

Check out the 'Critical Reading Specimen Question Paper' for examples of the type of questions you could be faced with in your exam at www.brightredbooks.net/N5English.

ONLINE TEST

Take the '*Bold Girls*: How to answer' test online at www.brightredbooks.net/N5English.

RONA MUNRO, *BOLD GIRLS*: SOME WAYS OF ANSWERING (CONTD)

QUESTION 4: HINTS FOR AN ANSWER

You need to find words/phrases/expressions which tell you what was on each woman's mind, and then go on to say what the use of these words/phrases tells you about their concerns at the time. You will get marks for one quotation and a detailed comment, or for two quotations with more straightforward comments.

Oh, but he was well respected./They sang for him as well, do you remember./He's still missed

Nora's thoughts are all for the loss of Michael and awe at his great standing in the community. She makes no mention at all of Marie, Michael's widow, underlining the play's insistence on the dominance of the male in this society, even in death. (2)

'Marie [...] never told a soul till we came in to her./Just sitting by the fire and the fire dead for hours and the baby crying and crying .../Her just sitting there.'

Cassie remembers not Michael's death itself but the effect on Marie, whose grief seems to touch her much more deeply. Her only reference to Michael is *He was popular, I'll say that for him.* This suggests that she will acknowledge his popularity but nothing else, hinting that she does not share Nora's admiration for the man. (2)

QUESTION 5: HINTS FOR ANSWER

A question like this underlines what we said earlier: you really need to know your Scottish texts so that you can refer to other passages where you saw a similar example of this technique at work. To help you out here, we make some suggestions which you should check out in detail for yourself.

So, what is this technique? From your reading of the play and the questions you have been answering, you will probably have worked out that these women from time to time talk at cross-purposes to each other; all three may talk a great deal, but they are not always listening to each other, or are deliberately ignoring each other. This tells us a great deal about the isolation that marks their lives – a major theme of the play.

There are probably three main instances of this technique at work in the play. These can be found on the following pages: pp. 2–3, p. 42, p. 46.

pp. 2–3

This is the first example of the technique in the play.

This technique is used for humorous effect here, but it establishes early on that these three women, though close in some ways, are not always on the same wavelength. Nora is concerned with the shortcomings of her washing powder; Marie is peeling potatoes; Cassie is teasing Marie about her underwear. The effect here is amusing, but all three are established as having very different interests, preoccupied as they are by very different concerns. This technique is very effective in suggesting, humorously here, that this trio might not be as close as they may appear.

p. 42

Here the women appear to be enjoying a night out at the club. Marie is engaged in a *'The Price-is-Right'* game with the compère while Nora and Cassie sit on the sidelines. Nora is talking of the identity of the mother of her boy's child; Cassie is busy shouting

Photo from the 2003 production of 'Bold Girls', at 29th Street Rep, New York.

game-playing advice to Marie, interrupted only by resentful references to how her mother always fed Cassie's brother before Cassie. Neither is listening to the other. Or perhaps they are deliberately ignoring each other's concerns and comments? This is an effective scene in that it serves to highlight the lack of connection – and underlying hostility – between mother and daughter.

p. 46

Later, in the club, Nora begins one of her tales of how she was assaulted by a soldier in the past; Cassie flirts with the man opposite, inviting Marie to enjoy a song with her; Marie is reduced to making polite noises. The girls' night out, far from bonding them, serves gradually to mark for the audience the distance between the women and their concerns. On each occasion, as in the minute's silence, it becomes clear that all three live very different lives, maintaining very different values; and their fundamental isolation, one from another, lies very close under the surface of their relations. Such an approach by Munro is highly effective in signalling to the audience this dislocation.

THINGS TO DO AND THINK ABOUT

Success in these types of question involves much more than having a sound understanding of characters and themes, important though that is. A play is a living entity, so you need to be secure in the sequence of events, how each scene throws light on the developing situation between the characters and how characters themselves reveal different aspects of themselves. A good way to do this is to make scene-by-scene notes for each character as you read. These could form the basis of four useful group discussions, one for each scene of the play. The more you talk about these people, the better you get to know them.

ONLINE TEST

Take the '*Bold Girls*: How to answer' test online at www. brightredbooks.net/N5English

ONLINE

Listen to Rona Munro talking about one of her other plays, *Iron*, by following the 'Rona Munro on Woman's Hour' link at www.brightredbooks.net/N5English

DON'T FORGET

To maximise your score in the high-value final question, *know* your text in great detail. That means *many* readings in your own time.

ANNE DONOVAN, *HIEROGLYPHICS AND OTHER STORIES*

Originally from Coatbridge, Anne Donovan studied English and Philosophy at Glasgow University before becoming an English teacher. She taught in various secondary schools until 2003 when, after the publication of her first novel, she made the transition to full-time writing.

Her collection *Hieroglyphics and Other Stories* was published in 2001 to considerable critical and popular acclaim. In 2003, the publication of her first novel *Buddha Da* was followed soon after by its inclusion on the shortlist of potential winners of the prestigious Orange Prize for Fiction. It was later nominated for the Whitbread First Novel Award, sealing Anne Donovan's place as one of the leading writers of her generation. The same year saw Donovan adapting the short story *Hieroglyphics* into a one-act play which was staged at Oran Mor in Glasgow and later published in an ASLS anthology, *Plays for Schools*.

DON'T FORGET

The page references in this section are from Canongate's 2004 edition of *Hieroglyphics and Other Stories*!

ONLINE

Check out 'Wiki: Anne Donovan' or 'Books from Scotland: Anne Donovan' for more background at www.brightredbooks.net/N5English

VIDEO LINK

For a short dramatisation of parts of this story and interview with Anne Donovan, check out 'BBC: All That Glisters' at www.brightredbooks.net/N5English

OUTLINE AND THEMES

The anthology consists of 18 short stories, 11 of them written in Glaswegian Scots with a twelfth alternating between Standard English and Glaswegian Scots. All, with the exception of one, are told in a female voice; six of them (and part of a seventh) are voiced by a young girl, two by elderly women.

The collection follows female experience from childhood to old age: the first six explore the world through young girls' eyes; the seventh bridges the child/woman divide; the following four depict various mother/child relationships; the later ones focus on various aspects of adult relationships, with the final two highlighting the world of older women.

YOUR SELECTION

The six short stories you are asked to explore in National 5 offer a good cross-section of Anne Donovan's concerns in this anthology. To help you spot the links between them, here is an outline guide to some of the recurring ideas, themes and relationships which connect them.

'All that Glisters'

This is the first of several stories foregrounding the relationship between a young girl and her parent(s), a thematic link in the collection. The girl, who throughout is associated with light (Clare, being a corruption of the French word for 'light') and colour, brings with her a sparkle and brightness to her dying father. Once a ghostly figure in his white asbestos-covered clothes, he is now drained of all colour in his own life, cheered only by the colour his daughter brings him. The story celebrates the colour and spontaneity of young people in the face of the darker, more prosaic world of adults.

contd

'Virtual Pals'

Here two 12-year-old girls, one on Earth, the other on Jupiter, exchange e-mails detailing facts of their respective lives. Although Glasgow-based Siobhan writes in Standard English most of the time, some expressions derive from Glaswegian Scots, causing Jupiter-based Irina minor translation problems. Here Donovan is humorously satirising, through Irina's 'other world' comments, the lack of confidence that many Scottish teenage girls have in themselves and in their own native language.

'Dear Santa'

This is another story featuring the parent/child relationship, this time that of a mother and her 8-year-old daughter, Alison, the narrator. Here, communication between them has broken down due to the mother's preference for the younger sibling, Katie. In her unhappiness, Alison cannot articulate her feelings to the mother she adores.

'A Chitterin Bite'

Here the Scots-language issue, touched on lightly in 'Virtual Pals', is again highlighted, this time as one means of characterising Mary Henderson. By switching backwards and forwards in time and place, and between Glaswegian Scots and Standard English, Donovan depicts how a warm, loving young girl can grow up into a rather cold, brittle woman due to an unhappy childhood incident.

'Away in a Manger'

Once again, Anne Donovan revisits the mother/child relationship. This time it takes on a new poignancy, as the Christmas setting ends with Sandra and Amy adopting a quasi-Madonna and Child position on their journey home. Although a kindly and protective mother, Sandra seems cut off from the broader humanity of the child, who reaches out emotionally to the homeless young man they find asleep in the nativity crèche. The child seems intuitively to understand the real spirit of Christmas in a way that is denied to the worldlier adult.

'Zimmerobics'

Here Donovan explores the inter-generational lack of understanding again, this time not in a mother/daughter relationship but between elderly aunt and niece. Challenged by old age, declining mobility and a somewhat unloving, albeit superficially caring, niece, Miss Knight, through zimmerobics, triumphs, at least temporarily, over her various adversities to find happiness as she moves, finally, in the last lines of the story 'in perfect time to the music'.

ONLINE TEST

Take the '*Hieroglyphics and Other Stories* by Anne Donovan' test online at www.brightredbooks.net/N5English

THINGS TO DO AND THINK ABOUT

As you read these stories, look out for the links that may connect them. These might derive from use of the Scots language, explorations of family relationships, communication between parents and children or the spontaneous freshness of a child's view of experience. But Anne Donovan provides here a rich reading experience – so, as you read, be aware that these links are not the only ones. Be prepared to make connections of your own in this collection of fascinating characters and situations.

ANNE DONOVAN: GETTING TO GRIPS WITH THE TEXT

'AWAY IN A MANGER'

In this extract from 'Away in a Manger', Sandra and her daughter, Amy, visit George Square, Glasgow, to see the Christmas lights. Amy discovers more than the baby Jesus in the nativity crèche. As you read, keep in mind what the spirit of Christmas is supposed to be all about and the differences in the ways in which Amy and her mother react to the stranger.

This year the nativity scene was bigger than life-sized. The figures were bronze statues, staunin on a carpet of straw and surrounded by what looked like a hoose made of glass. It was placed tae wan side of the square, inside a fence. Sandra thought it was quite dull lookin. Weans liked bright colours and these huge people were kind of scary. She minded the wee plastic figures of Mary and Joseph she used tae set carefully in place every Christmas, leavin the baby Jesus tae last. They'd fitted intae the palm of her haund. She'd need tae get a crib for Amy. Sandra wisnae very religious, no religious at all, really, but still, it was nice for wee ones tae have a crib.

'Is that the manger, Mammy?' Amy pointed.

'That's right. D'you know who all the people are?'

Amy sucked at her mitt and looked carefully at the figures. 'That's Mary and that's Joseph – and that's the baby Jesus. And that's a shepherd wi his sheep. But who's that, Mammy?'

'They're the three wise kings. Look – they've got presents for the baby Jesus.'

'But who's *that*, Mammy? Behind the cow.'

Huddled in the straw, hidden in a corner behind the figure of a large beast, lay a man. He was slightly built, dressed in auld jeans and a thin jacket. One of his feet stuck round the end of the statue and on it was a worn trainin shoe, the cheapest kind they sold in the store. Sandra moved round tae get a better look at him. He was quite young, wi a pointed face and longish dark hair. A stubbly growth covered his chin. He seemed sound asleep.

'Is he an angel, Mammy?'

Sandra didnae answer. She was lookin at the glass structure wonderin how on earth

contd

he'd got in. One of the panels at the back looked a bit loose, but you'd think they'd have an alarm on it. Lucky for him they never – at least he'd be warm in there. She was that intent on the glass panels that she'd nearly forgotten he wisnae a statue. Suddenly he opened his eyes. They were grey.

Amy grabbed her mother's arm and started jumpin up and down.

'Mammy, look, he's alive! Look Mammy. He's an angel!'

'Naw, he's no an angel. He's a man.'

'But, Mammy, what's he daein in there wi the baby Jesus?'

'Ah don't know, Amy. Some folk don't have anywhere tae stay.'

Sandra didnae want her tae know, she was too young. She wished she could have thought of a story – he's a security guard havin a sleep, he's a councillor checkin how they've spent the ratepayers' money, he's an art student examining the statues.

Amy stared at the man, her head tae one side. 'He could come and stay wi us.'

'Naw, he cannae.'

'How no?'

'Because we havenae got room.'

'We have so, Mammy, we've got a spare room.'

'Aye but that's where your granny sleeps when she comes tae stay. She's comin for Christmas soon.'

'Ah can sleep wi Granny. Ah like sleepin wi ma granny. She's fat.'

'Don't tell her that.'

'How no? She's like a big hot-water bottle.'

Sandra laughed. 'C'mon.'

She took Amy's haund but Amy stayed where she was.

'If ah slept wi ma granny the man could have ma bed.'

'Naw, he couldnae. Ye cannae just take anybody intae your hoose. We don't know him.'

'If he came tae stay wi us we would know him.'

'Once and for all, he's no comin hame wi us. And if you don't stop gaun on aboot it Santa'll no come this year either.' She took Amy by the haund and led her away oot the square.

ONLINE

Find out more about homelessness in Scotland by following the 'Homelessness Statistics' link at www.brightredbooks.net/N5English

ONLINE TEST

Take the 'Anne Donovan: Getting to grips with the text' test online at www.brightredbooks.net/N5English

QUESTIONS

1 Summarise what happens in this extract from the short story. Make at least four key points. **4**

2 Look at the first paragraph. Sandra feels that this nativity crèche is not at all that it should be. Show how this is revealed through word choice. **2**

3 Choose two examples of Anne Donovan's use of language which help to show Sandra in a good light as a caring mother. **2**

4 With close reference to the text, explain the reactions to the young man of:
(a) Sandra
(b) Amy **4**

5 By referring to the ideas or narrative style of this short story, show how it is similar to *or* different from other short stories by Anne Donovan you have read. **8**

20 marks total

THINGS TO DO AND THINK ABOUT

Have a look at the questions above and think how you would go about trying to answer them. Find hints and suggestions on the next page.

ANNE DONOVAN: WORKING OUT YOUR RESPONSE

Remember, when you see phrases like 'Show how this is revealed through word choice' or 'Choose two examples of Anne Donovan's language' or 'With close reference to the text ...', the examiners are looking for precise words or phrases, so it is your eye for detail that will bring success. Intelligent generalities will not.

Your experience answering the questions on *Bold Girls* should have helped you to feel more confident about setting out to answer these Anne Donovan questions. Here are some worked answers to them. Check out your own answers to see how you got on.

QUESTION 1

You need to make four points here. One mark for each point.

- Sandra and Amy are visiting the nativity crèche
- Sandra compares this year's large figures unfavourably with the ones of her childhood
- In identifying the nativity figures, Amy notices one extra
- Amy mistakes the sleeping young man for an angel
- Sandra explains he is homeless
- Amy's instinct is to invite him to use their spare room
- Sandra refuses, making the excuse that it is needed for family use

If you set out your answer clearly, the examiner can be in no doubt that you have duly produced four points.

QUESTION 2

You will usually get your two marks with two examples and detailed comments.

- 'quite dull lookin' – suggests it lacks the colour she expected
- 'kind of scary' – inappropriately frightening for a Christmas crèche

QUESTION 3

Remember that 'use of language' allows you a wide choice of features to remark on. Two examples with detailed comments will get you full marks; less developed comments will need three or four examples.

- 'She'd need to get a crib for Amy' – feels her responsibility towards her daughter
- 'nice for weans tae have a crib' – generous-spirited to the young
- 'didnae want her to know' – protective in instincts
- Sentence structure: she lists in her head a range of silly/improbable reasons for the man's presence to shield Amy from the truth of homelessness

QUESTION 4

'Close reference to the text' reminds you that your comments need to be firmly grounded in words/expressions/ phrases you have selected carefully from the text to illustrate your comments.

Sandra:

- 'wonderin how on earth he'd got in' – curious/puzzled by his method of entry
- 'nearly forgotten he wisnae a statue' – not fully conscious of his human state
- 'at least he'd be warm in there' – relieved by his physical comfort
- 'cannae just take anybody intae your hoose' – rejection of strangers

contd

Amy:

- 'Is he an angel?' – readiness to accept him as a holy figure
- 'he could come and stay wi us' – spontaneously generous, welcoming
- 'we've got a spare room – practical thinking
- 'the man could have ma bed' – selfless response
- 'If he came tae stay [...] we would know him – seeks to reason her mother out of her objections

QUESTION 5

In choosing either ideas or narrative style to write about, you should make at least one fully detailed point on either side of how this story is similar to, and one equally detailed point on how it is different from, ideas or narrative style in other of Donovan's short stories. Less detailed points will need to be more numerous. Some possible approaches are listed below, but they are by no means the only ones possible.

Similar ideas:

- Amy, like Clare in 'All that Glisters', challenges conventional grown-up thinking about life (and death) as they encounter it. Amy, unlike her mother, sees it as perfectly natural to welcome strangers into her home; Clare, unlike her aunt, sees it as perfectly natural to observe her father's passing with the bright colours he liked in life. Neither girl has been affected by adult prejudices/conventions about acceptable behaviour.
- This story and 'Dear Santa' explore a mother/daughter relationship around Christmas and highlight the difficulties/issues this season brings. It is the season of 'goodwill to all men', a commodity which is lacking in different ways in each of these stories: Sandra fails to reach out to the homeless; Alison's mother fails to reach out to her daughter.
- This story explores problems of communicating between generations, as do 'Dear Santa' and 'Zimmerobics'. Each generation seems on a different emotional wavelength to the other. One side seems to have a limited understanding of the thinking/feelings of the other.

Different ideas:

- Here we have a loving mother, highly protective of her small daughter (although she does not fully understand or respond to her concerns about the homeless). In 'Dear Santa', we have a rather cold mother who does not demonstrate the same protective instincts as Sandra, exposing Alison regularly to unfavourable comments with regard to her little sister, Katie.
- In 'Away in a Manger', Sandra and Amy seem to exist in a world of their own – whatever their differences of opinion about the homeless man – as they journey cuddled together 'intae the dark night', isolated from the rest of the world and yet together. In 'Dear Santa', Alison exists in a family and social network (mother, father, sister, nativity play), yet, in her inability to share her secret sorrow, is totally alone.

Similar narrative style:

- Glaswegian Scots is used in both narrative and dialogue here to bring alive the mother/daughter relationship, as it is in 'Dear Santa'.

Different narrative style:

- In the mother/daughter relationship in 'Dear Santa', we have the relationship seen through the eyes of the daughter, Alison. We are not given direct insight into the mother's thoughts; we can only assess her feelings (or lack of them) by Alison's reporting. In 'Away in a Manger', the narration is largely by the mother, Sandra, although we learn quite a lot about Amy, too, from her lively, spontaneous comments.

DON'T FORGET

Never lose sight of the fact that 'with close reference to the text' means just that. Ground your answers in items taken from the text itself, and then add your comment on the word/words selected: '... suggests that .../ gives the impression that ...'. No vague general statements here, please!

ONLINE TEST

Take the 'Anne Donovan: Working out your response' test online at www. brightredbooks.net/ N5English.

ONLINE

Check out 'The Short Review – *Hieroglyphics and Other Stories*' for another perspective on the collection at www.brightredbooks.net/ N5English.

THINGS TO DO AND THINK ABOUT

How did you fare in question 5? This is the first time where you had to link your appreciation of *this* text to another text altogether. You will have seen that, to answer this high-value question successfully in the exam, you really need to know your short stories very well indeed. In the exam, you won't have the texts in front of you to look back for similarities and differences as you do now!

EDWIN MORGAN

MORGAN: THE MAN

Born in 1920 in Hyndland, part of Glasgow's West End, and later brought up in Pollokshields and Rutherglen, Edwin Morgan attended Rutherglen Academy and Glasgow High School before entering Glasgow University in 1937. He read English Language and Literature there until his studies were interrupted by the Second World War, when he enrolled as a conscientious objector in the Royal Army Medical Corps.

He returned from service in Egypt, Palestine and the Lebanon to complete his degree with First Class Honours. On graduating, he took up a post at the university, where he taught until he retired in 1980 as titular professor of English to devote the rest of his life to writing. He was the recipient of many honours, including the Queen's Gold Medal for Poetry in 2000. He was appointed Scotland's first 'Scots Makar' of modern times, the Scottish equivalent of Poet Laureate, in 2004. He died in 2010.

MORGAN: THE POET

Morgan was among the most inventive, adventurous poets of his age, seeing poetry 'as an instrument of exploration, like a spaceship, into new fields of feeling or experience' in his introduction to his selection in *Worlds* (Penguin Education, 1974). The poems you study for National 5 give only a minuscule indication of the depth and breadth of his output. In terms of forms, he was equally at home in writing in the centuries-old tradition of the sonnet as he was in daring experiments in 'concrete' poetry, where the shape of the words on the page is as vital in conveying the poem's intended effect as the meaning of the words themselves.

EXAMPLE:

Here is an example of Morgan's concrete style at its most playful. The poem is called 'Siesta of a Hungarian Snake'. This is the whole poem.

s sz **sz SZ sz SZ sz Zs sz ZS sz** zs z

In terms of language, he ranges widely from Glaswegian Scots to attempts to create the language of the Loch Ness Monster, men from Mercury, Hungarian snakes or even an African hyena – this last being the speaker in a poem for study here. Giving a voice to all kinds of perhaps unlikely creatures forms part of Morgan's broad, all-encompassing humanity. 'I feel the whole world is able to express something', he told Marshall Walker in a 1977 interview. Complementing this desire to give a voice to others is a drive to intensify the power of his own, often through a series of complex verbal effects – a process which appears to have fascinated him and which we see at work in several of the poems for study here. In terms of topics, he ranges widely, often finding material in his native Glasgow or in the history and geography of Scotland, but also venturing into the worlds of computers, interplanetary travel, Bible history or even pre-history.

VIDEO LINK ●

Follow the link 'Off the page: Edwin Morgan', at www.brightredbooks.net/N5English, for a very useful 25-minute film in which Morgan discusses his life and the development of his writing. He also reads some of his own poetry, against the background of Great Western Road, Glasgow, mentioned in the poem 'Winter' here.

THE POEMS

'Good Friday'

There is a 'me' in this poem, presumably Morgan himself, who restricts himself to giving the time and place of the encounter; but the poem is essentially a dramatic monologue by a cheerily drunken man who, in the course of a brief bus journey along Bath Street in Glasgow, comments on Christ's crucifixion and resurrection, the meaning of Easter, his own drinking habits, lack of education and immediate intentions. At what is usually a time on Good Friday (3pm) when, historically, a darkness was said to cover the land, this Glasgow Good Friday is bathed in sunshine, and the drunk is happily celebrating and

contd

off to buy Easter eggs for the 'kiddies'. Morgan captures faithfully the speech patterns of the new passenger, partly by the use of repeated phrases and partly by statements which don't quite hang together grammatically. Morgan has a keen ear for how tipsy people often have to struggle to express themselves. The drunk man's speech, like the bus itself, is given to lurches and sudden changes of direction. Note how Morgan avoids any direct comment on his fellow traveller but listens without comment, seeming to find the man's chatter harmlessly amusing, even picturing his descent from the top deck in 'concrete' terms, with a word for each descending step.

'Hyena'

Here we have Morgan giving a voice to an unlikely and, by normal standards, a highly unattractive creature, the hyena, scavenger of the African bush. From line one, the hyena tells readers he is waiting for us – and, from his later confessions, there can be only one end to the encounter. His aim is

> *[...] to pick you clean*

> *And leave your bones to the wind.*

Yet Morgan goes out of his way to bring an energy and vitality to the hyena with a series of vivid similes and metaphors which bring us close to the predator whose avowed intent, let us not forget, is to devour us. He adds to the beast's proximity to us by having him insinuate himself into our conscientiousness by interrogating us directly. Morgan frequently uses enjambment to give – horrifically – a conversational tone to the hyena's vicious intentions as he addresses us. The relentless repetition of *I am …* adds a hypnotic chant-like quality to his address. While the poem is at one level a strikingly vivid portrayal of a hyena addressing us in its own monologue, we might also see it as a comment on human fascination with the hypnotic power of what we often know to be dangerous and destructive. Like the hyena, we too might be *the slave of darkness*. Here, Morgan absents himself totally; he simply asks us to observe and contemplate.

'In the Snack Bar'

Here, as in 'Good Friday', we have another casual Glasgow encounter. There are, however, sharp differences: this time the effect is far from cheery and light-hearted as before; this time the speaker, again presumably Morgan, plays an active part in the events of the poem, commenting directly on the action and his response to it. In a detailed realisation of a 'crowded evening snack-bar' with its formica, hissing coffee machine and fixed stools, the old man is presented almost as a species from another world, *like a monstrous animal caught in a tent/In some story*. The speaker helps the old man go to the toilet. Skilfully, Morgan captures the slow progress of the pair as they descend the stairs to the toilet by effective use of repetition and inversion:

> *And slowly we go down. And slowly we go down.*

This is a technique which Morgan returns to several times in the poem to mirror the man's painfully slow progress in carrying out any action. His helplessness and clumsiness in coping with the simplest action is frequently further underlined by Morgan's word choice: *he shambles uncouth, he clings to me, to haul his blind hump*. Morgan is not only an active, compassionate helper here (one whose strength serves to emphasise the frailty of the old man) but also a moved, distraught commentator:

> *Dear Christ, to be born for this!*

THINGS TO DO AND THINK ABOUT

Follow the link to 'Screenr – Hyena by Edwin Morgan' at http://www.screenr.com/sCV to hear Morgan himself reading this poem. Alternatively, try to find the ASLS-issued CD, *17 Poems by Edwin Morgan*, which also has 'Trio' and 'In the Snack Bar' with a commentary by Professor Roderick Watson.

DON'T FORGET

In class, you will be reading these poems from the various Morgan collections. For your own revision purposes, it might be useful to type them out. In this way, you can underline/highlight words and phrases and connect them to your notes in the margin. Revising will be that much easier when you have notes/comments/quotations all side by side.

ONLINE TEST

Take the 'Edwin Morgan' test online at www.brightredbooks.net/N5English

EDWIN MORGAN: THE POEMS (CONTD)

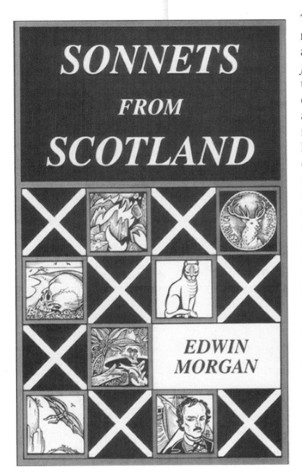

'Slate'

This is the first of the six poems we are looking at here which is not written in free verse, i.e. poetry which avoids regular **rhythm** and **rhyme**. 'Slate' is the first in Morgan's sonnet sequence *Sonnets from Scotland*. A sonnet is a 14-line poetic form which Morgan uses here in its Italian (or Petrarchan) form, as it is sometimes called, which consists of an 8-line section (or octave) followed by a 6-line section (or sestet). We see there is a carefully observed rhyme scheme of *abba, cddc, efg, efg*. Here Morgan cleverly hides the skill with which he has put the sonnet together, by camouflaging the rhymes at the end of the lines. This is done by pushing the completion of one line's sense onto the next one. As a result, on a casual first reading, this use of enjambment may well result in the sound of many of these rhymes being lost. Readers are invited to follow their eye rather than their ear. This blurring of pronounced rhymes gives an almost conversational tone to this most formally organised poem.

From the Glasgow of 'Good Friday' and 'In the Snack Bar', we have moved from everyday encounters to the wild and violent geological formation of Scotland itself, as seen, it seems, by a rather mysterious long-lived 'we', far in the future or perhaps from another world, underlining the breadth of Morgan's subject matter as well as poetic vision. This all-seeing 'we' witnessed the founding of Scotland's geology, with no other people around to see it. Its reference to

> *Memory of men! That was to come*

suggests that it is almost as if the human race had already departed. The poem's final words celebrate the terrain of Scotland which, with its rugged 'flint, chalk, slate', endures. This is a far from conventional viewing of Scotland, emphasising as it does its geological rather than historical past.

'Trio'

DON'T FORGET

These six poems differ greatly in topics and techniques. Make sure your notes are sufficiently full to allow you to make contrasts and parallels between all six.

While 'In the Snack Bar' records the darker side of city life in Glasgow, in 'Trio' we see Morgan delighting mightily in a casual encounter in Buchanan Street one 'sharp winter evening' just before Christmas. Here the speaker, like the drunk man in 'Good Friday', appears to have doubts as to the credibility of the Christian myth (*Whether Christ is born, or not born* ...). Nevertheless, there is no doubting the sheer joy that the trio of two young girls and a young man inspire in the speaker as he describes in great detail their sighting, the gifts they carry and the *cloud of happiness* that surrounds them. Morgan is here cleverly using these three young people and their surroundings to draw modern-day parallels with the three kings of the Christmas legend: they carry gifts, not the gold, frankincense and myrrh of the Magi, but a guitar, baby and chihuahua; they appear, not under a star but under the Christmas lights of Buchanan Street; a child, too, is central to the encounter.

The speaker dips into yet another myth (of Orpheus and his lute) to salute in mock-heroic terms the mistletoe of the guitar-carrying young man as an *Orphean sprig*, hailing also the baby and chihuahua in equally delighted exclamations of joy. This happiness may be the outcome of a commercially driven Christmas rather than a

contd

religiously inspired one, but the speaker sees it having the power, no less than a Christian one, to drive away the gloom of *the vale of tears* which is the world, and which *abdicates/under the Christmas lights.* It is a joy which lingers even after they have passed out of sight, marking the *end of this winter's day.*

Morgan employs a contrast of styles here: in the early lines his language is matter-of-fact, conversational in its use of enjambment and simple word choice to describe the physical appearance of the trio. When we get to *Orphean sprig!*, Morgan changes tone as he seeks to underline for us the significance he places on this encounter. Out goes the everyday, descriptive language he used earlier to describe the street scene, to be replaced by language which sounds a grander and loftier note. By this switch of language, he seeks to draw our attention to the power of casual incidents like this one to give a real and lasting uplift to the people observing them.

'Winter'

Here Morgan exploits his English lecturer's knowledge of Tennyson's 1833 poem 'Tithonus', a man who in Greek mythology sought immortality but forgot to wish for eternal youth as well. Tennyson's poem begins:

> *The woods decay, the woods decay and fall,*
> *The vapours weep their burthen to the ground,*
> *Man comes and tills the field and lies beneath,*
> *And after many a summer dies the swan.*

Tithonus is, consequently, left as a lonely, solitary character, a fate which seems to be shared by the speaker here as, at the end of the poem, he gazes at the *grey dead pane.* Is that *pane* a play on 'pain'? Morgan moves the season on from autumn to full winter and the context from Greek myth to Great Western Road.

By altering the punctuation of the original poem, Morgan achieves a completely different effect from that of Tennyson. Gone is the smoothly flowing, gentle sadness of the Tennyson poem. The shortened phrases lead to jerky forward movement which creates a fractured, pained effect. The pain we understand better when we learn that Morgan was writing at a time when he had lost people close to him. This is a raw winter of the soul as well as of the calendar. This halting, difficult progress continues in the fragmented phrases with which Morgan describes the frozen winter scene, insisting, in addition, on the language of hardness and sharpness as in *swan-white glints only crystal beyond white.* This is intensified as the *stark scene* is *cut* by *cries in the warring air* and the *hiss of blades.* The harshness of the alliteration and onomatopoeia only add to the bleakness.

Gradually, the skaters disappear into the fog as, eventually, do the lights themselves. Now the scene is left to the fog which takes over and *drives monstrous down the dual carriageway* like some demonic driver, leaving the speaker solitary, staring blankly at only greyness. And greyness stares back at him. In its rich poetic effects which underline the bleaker aspects of winter, this is a poem in which the speaker's emotions seem as frozen as the external landscape.

ONLINE

Discover more about Edwin Morgan and his poems by clicking 'Scottish Poetry Library: Edwin Morgan Archive' at www.brightredbooks.net/N5English

ONLINE TEST

Take the 'Edwin Morgan: The Poems' test online at www.brightredbooks.net/N5English

THINGS TO DO AND THINK ABOUT

In these six poems, we have only seen a fraction of Morgan's inventive creativity. Nevertheless, we have seen at work an interesting cross-section of topics and styles at various times in his life: the world of Glasgow (dark as well as life-enhancing), the world of nature in vastly varying treatments ('Hyena', 'Slate' and 'Winter'); formal sonnet form and free verse, simple conversational tone and more elaborated use of language. Keep all these cross-currents alive in your head as you read and prepare to answer questions.

EDWIN MORGAN: GETTING TO GRIPS WITH THE TEXT

Once you have read over the poem and come to terms with what you think Morgan's intended effect might be, ask yourself how it resembles and/or differs from the other five poems you are now familiar with. Yes, it is a 'Glasgow' poem, but about a character very different from the one encountered in 'In the Snack Bar' and with a very different response from the speaker. There is also a connection with a Christian festival, as in 'Trio', but does the speaker seem to draw the same response from the encounter? And style? Are there other poems which share the same approach to language?

ONLINE

For more resources on Morgan, check out 'Education Scotland: Edwin Morgan poems' at www. brightredbooks.net/ N5English.

'GOOD FRIDAY' BY EDWIN MORGAN

Three o'clock. The bus lurches

Round into the sun. 'D's this go –'

He flops beside me – 'right along Bath Street?

– Oh tha's, tha's all right, see I've

Got to get some Easter eggs for the kiddies.

I've had a wee drink, ye understand –

Ye'll maybe think it's a – funny day

To be celebrating – well, no, but ye see

I wasny working, and I like to celebrate

When I'm no working – I don't say it's right

I'm no saying it's right, ye understand – ye understand?

But anyway tha's the way I look at it –

I'm no boring you, heh? – ye see today,

Take today, I don't know what today's in aid of,

Whether Christ was – crucified or was he –

Rose fae the dead like, see what I mean?

You're an educatit man, he jist canny – jist

Hasny got it, know what I mean,

He's jist bliddy ignorant – Christ aye,

Bliddy ignorant. Well –' The bus brakes violently,

He lunges for the stair, swings down-off,

Into the sun for his Easter eggs,

On very

      Nearly

          Steady

             Legs.

QUESTIONS

Have a look at the following questions and think how you would go about trying to answer them. Find hints and suggestions on the next page.

1   In your own words, summarise those aspects of the tipsy man's character which emerge in the course of the bus ride. Make at least four key points.   4

2   With close reference to the text, identify two ways in which Morgan signals that this man is not entirely sober.   2

3   Show how two examples of the poet's use of language effectively convey the idea of a bus journey.   2

4   What is the atmosphere created by the writer? How does the writer's use of language create this mood?   2

5   How effective do you find the poem's final four lines? Your answer might deal with ideas and/or language.   2

6   With close textual reference, show how the ideas/and or language of this poem are similar to *or* different from another poem by Morgan which you have read.   8

20 marks total

THINGS TO DO AND THINK ABOUT

By now, you should be getting into the habit of supporting your answers to these types of question with carefully selected evidence from the text. You may have a perfectly intelligent and sensitive response to the poem, but if it is not backed up by detailed references to the text (where requested) or in your own words (where requested), you will fail to achieve the marks you are aiming for. Make sure, too, that you take note of the marks which each question carries, and judge your time appropriately.

EDWIN MORGAN: WORKING OUT YOUR RESPONSE

QUESTION 1 - HINTS FOR AN ANSWER

Your key points here on the man's character will need to be founded on sharply observed detail which Morgan is generous in supplying. Here are some key points you might make, with (to help you in other similar questions) the textual evidence from which the points are derived.

Textual evidence	Key points to be made
1 *Got to get some Easter eggs for the kiddies*	Generous in his instincts (1)
2 *I like to celebrate / When I'm no working*	Enjoys himself when he has free time (1)
3 *I'm no saying it's right, ye understand – ye understand?*	Keen that people should understand him (1)
4 *I'm no boring you, heh?*	Sensitive to other people's feelings (1)
5 *bliddy ignorant*	Honest about his lack of knowledge (1)
6 *You're an educatit man*	Shows respect for education (1)
7 *Whether Christ was – crucified or was he –*	Vague about religious matters (1)

QUESTION 2 - HINTS FOR AN ANSWER

There are various ways of tackling this question. Two obvious ways would be to look at word choice and/or sentence structure to indicate how Morgan signals how much the man has had to drink.

Word Choice

'*flops*' suggests that he has no control of his body/collapses in a heap.

'*lunges*' suggests that his movement is violent and sudden/not premeditated.

'*swings down*' suggests unsteady descent/swaying from side to side.

'*very nearly steady*' suggests that his control of movement is not entirely secure.

Sentence Structure

Repetition: '– *Oh tha's, tha's*' indicates he is struggling to find his words.

Repetition: '*ye see today,*

Take today, I don't know what today's in aid of'

needless repetition suggests not sure of where the sentence is going.

There are other instances of needless repetition, indicating a verbal insecurity as a result of his drinking.

He never appears able to complete sentences; he speaks in fragments, his brain obviously fuddled by alcohol.

He also changes the subject of his sentence midway:

'*I don't know ...*

He's jist bliddy ignorant'

suggests that he has lost the thread of what he was trying to say, referring to himself both as 'I' and 'He'.

QUESTION 3 – HINTS FOR AN ANSWER

Here word choice is probably the most useful aspect of language to examine.

- 'bus lurches' suggests a sudden, unstable movement as it rounds corner.
- 'brakes violently' suggests abrupt, destabilising effect on passengers.

QUESTION 4 – HINTS FOR AN ANSWER

There is a general feeling of good-natured happiness (not what we expect on the day marking Christ's crucifixion). The 'Good' of the poem's title here really has its literal meaning, rather than the conventional religious one.

'into the sun' is repeated at the start and end of the poem, suggesting warmth and brightness (the reverse of the darkness which the Bible tells us covered the land at three o'clock).

'I like to celebrate

When I'm no working'

suggests the infectious holiday mood created by the man.

'Got to get some Easter eggs for the kiddies' suggests generosity/wanting to give pleasure to others.

ONLINE TEST

Take the 'Edwin Morgan: Working out your response' test online at www. brightredbooks.net/ N5English.

QUESTION 5 – HINTS FOR AN ANSWER

From a careful analysis of the text, you will by now have noticed that Morgan has been most effective in conveying the idea of a rather rough, bouncy bus ride and the cheery but chaotic chat of the tipsy man. He rounds this off most effectively by these final four lines, which capture both the behaviour of the bus and the man.

'The bus brakes violently,

He lunges for the stairs'

is effective in that it reminds us that bus and man have been in a rather comically unsteady state throughout. Our last view of this cheery man is an amusing one, and quiet amusement seems to have been Morgan's reaction to the whole incident.

'On very

    Nearly

       Steady

         Legs'

By setting out the final line in this way, Morgan is picturing the unsteady descent of the man from the top deck, a line for every, slightly wobbly, footfall. This reminds us of Morgan's interest in 'concrete' poetry in which the shape of the poem on the page plays a key role in the poem's intended effect on the reader.

DON'T FORGET

Always check the number of marks on offer for each question and allocate your time accordingly.

 THINGS TO DO AND THINK ABOUT

To help you get to know these poems thoroughly, why not set up a few group discussions? In each session, take 2 poems and explore the similarities and contrasts. Allocate selected tasks to each member of the group. It could be the basis for an Outcome 2 for your Creation and Production unit, but more importantly, you will really get to grips with what is going on in each poem.

EDWIN MORGAN: WORKING OUT YOUR RESPONSE (CONTD)

QUESTION 6 – HINTS FOR AN ANSWER

In six poems of great richness, there are many points that could be made here. These are only a few which you might mention.

Similar ideas:

- Morgan's material for the poem comes from an encounter around the time of a Christian festival (Easter), as does his material for 'Trio' (set around Christmas).

- As in 'Trio' and 'In the Snack Bar', Morgan draws his inspiration from Glasgow street life.

- Like 'Hyena', 'Good Friday' is a dramatic monologue where the speaker is keen to get his views across to us.

contd

Different ideas:

- The speaker comments on his reaction to the encounter in 'Trio' (*'The vale of tears is powerless before you ...'*) and 'In the Snack Bar' (*'Dear Christ, to be born for this?'*), whereas here he (the poem's 'me') remains silent throughout the man's monologue.

- This brief encounter, like that in 'Trio', is centred around happiness; in 'Trio' there is the happiness of the young people, here the merriness of the tipsy man, whereas 'In the Snack Bar' foregrounds only sad compassion and despair.

- Like 'Hyena', this is a dramatic monologue, but the characters are wildly different in their personalities. In 'Good Friday', the man is concerned for others (*'Easter eggs for the kiddies'* and *'I'm no boring you, heh?'*), whereas here the hyena is wholly self-centred (*'My place is to pick you clean / And leave your bones to the wind'*).

- In 'Hyena', the main character is held up for our criticism. Here there appears to be no such intention; he seems viewed with amused tolerance.

Similar language:

- As in 'Hyena', the main character has a great desire to communicate and be understood by his hearers: *'– see what I mean?'* ('Good Friday'); *'What do you think of me?'* ('Hyena').

- As in 'Hyena', 'Trio', 'Winter' and 'In the Snack Bar', Morgan relies on the flexibility of free verse to help him articulate his response to very different situations.

Different language:

- In 'Good Friday', the speaker's words tumble out chaotically, often with sentences incomplete or with elements repeated, suggesting, amusingly, the unfocused verbal intentions of the speaker:

  'I don't know what today's in aid of,

  Whether Christ was – crucified or was he –

  Rose fae the dead like, see what I mean?'

- In 'Hyena', the speaker's language is highly articulate and rich in powerful metaphors and similes, the product of an organised, single-minded brain:

  'I sprawl as a shaggy bundle of gathered energy

  Like Africa sprawling in its waters.'

- When compared with 'Slate', we see the enormous breadth of Morgan's control of language. In 'Good Friday', we are presented with free verse, with fractured, often amusingly incomplete phrases in an unsteady rhythm which matches the unsteady state of the speaker's alcohol-bemused brain. In 'Slate', Morgan employs the highly formal structure of the sonnet to impose shape and form on the speech of the mysterious 'we' who comment with prophet-like solemnity on Scotland's birth.

DON'T FORGET

Remember what Alan Riach had to say at the beginning of this section about memorising poems you enjoy. There are many parts of the Morgan poems you have here which are easy and rewarding to memorise. How about a dramatised interpretation of the man on the bus? Memorising them would also be a very practical way of revising for the exam!

ONLINE

For more on Morgan, click 'Edwin Morgan: Official Site' at www.brightredbooks.net/N5English

ONLINE TEST

Take the 'Edwin Morgan: Working out your response' test online at www.brightredbooks.net/N5English

THINGS TO DO AND THINK ABOUT

Now you've reached the end of this section, you will have seen that to do well in the Scottish Literature context question in the exam, you will need to have an absolutely thorough knowledge of whatever text(s) you have been studying. This kind of knowledge cannot be achieved a few nights before the exam. Make sure that, in addition to work in class, you work steadily on them on your own, so that you can cope with making a multiplicity of links and contrasts when you are required to do so.

THE FOLIO

BETTER FOLIO-WRITING

By this stage in your studies, you are no stranger to essay-writing of all kinds. But, for National 5, you will need to ensure your writing has that added sparkle to maximise your final grade. So, how do you do that?

READ AROUND

The surest way to improve your writing style is to familiarise yourself with quality writing of all kinds: novels, short stories, biographies, travel writing and quality journalism are just a few genres to explore. By all means read for the pleasure they offer, but now is the moment to read quality texts with an added purpose: **to see what you can learn from professional writers**.

The gripping start to a story, the bringing to life of a character or setting, dialogue that crackles with realism: all these can profitably be studied for the improvement of your creative and reflective writing. The engagingly witty opening to an informative article, the usefulness of illustrative examples, the seamless transition from one paragraph to another: these are all aspects of quality journalism you can absorb to add persuasive conviction to your discursive texts. There is no shortage of models out there to study. Adopt a few ideas from the professionals, adapt them to suit your purpose – and you'll quickly see how your writing will progress!

WHAT DO I ALREADY KNOW?

Another way to raise your standards – one that's been right under your nose for some time – is to think about all the technical features you've been noting as you analyse Close Reading texts. So, how about bringing some of them into your own writing?

You're used to explaining the impact of minor sentences, inversion, metaphors, word choice, parallel structures to name only a few, so how about making all this hard-won information work for **you** in another context? We'll spend some time looking at this approach – but, before you even switch on the computer, you would do well to spend some time thinking over these practical considerations to get top grades.

TIPS FOR TOP GRADES

- **Does it interest me?** Do not even think about committing yourself to paper until you are sure what you are writing about is something that truly interests you. Whether it's a short story about a friendship that went wrong or an analysis of the future of renewable energy sources, spend plenty of time considering whether the core idea *really* interests you. Are you willing to spend many hours on this topic? If in doubt, the chances are it's the wrong choice. It will save a lot of time and effort in the long run if you do some hard thinking before you start.

- **Do I know about it?** Write from your existing knowledge base or about a topic you want to get to know about. If you don't know about deserted tropical islands, it's clearly not the setting for your short story – unless you want to do some serious research. Discursive writing will always need research. Are you sure how to get the most reliable, up-to-date information? And are you interested enough in the topic to **want** to set about getting it?

- **Do I have a plan?** Before even drafting a word, plan your ideas in rough. Use whatever method works for you: a mind-map, a listing of possibilities, a page of random brainstorming thoughts. Mull over them all, eventually discarding the non-starters before trying to organise the remaining ones into some rough outline of paragraph content and sequence.

- **Have I considered my audience?** You are not yet a professional writer who is writing exclusively to please yourself. Yes, of course you should enjoy your own writing, but remember you are also writing to impress examiners in a public exam. So, try to keep that in mind at all times. Crisp, clear prose which hangs together well and which offers a rich reading experience is what they are looking for. Indulge them.

- **Have I considered my purpose?** What are you setting out to do? Entertain? Persuade? Analyse? Whatever your ultimate aim, you need at all times to be examining your language to see if it is fulfilling the purpose you think it is. It is easy to set out on a persuasive tack and then discover that your language later on has become simply factual and informative. Keep checking that you are using the language appropriate for the task you have set yourself.

- **Is my plan working?** Yes, we all need a plan to get started, but, as your text progresses, are you noticing weaknesses or possibilities you didn't at first consider? Relax. It's a good sign, showing that you're beginning to think like a professional writer. Don't be scared to move paragraphs about, delete sentences, add phrases, discard a word to find a better one or whatever now seems necessary. With information technology, all this becomes relatively easy.

- **Is this the best I can do?** Don't get so lost in your story or analysis that you forget to check basic essentials. Before handing in any draft, make sure you proofread it to check the grammar, spelling, punctuation and vocabulary. Don't be caught out by basics like *its/it's*, *their/there*, *to/too* and so on. Mistakes like these indicate a lack of respect towards your own text – and towards the examiner, too.

ONLINE TEST

Check if your idea for your folio-writing piece ticks all the boxes online at www. brightredbooks.net/N5English

THINGS TO DO AND THINK ABOUT

The folio is the ideal place for people who feel that exams do not bring out the best in them. Here they can really show what they can do. So, consider folio choices carefully. This is where you can really bring up your grade. Think back over the kind of writing you have excelled in. Don't be in a hurry to decide on a topic or genre. Study the tips above as you try out a few ideas before settling on any one. Show results to friends to see how they react. It's not just any piece of writing; it's the most important piece you've tackled so far. Make it work for you.

WHAT SHOULD I WRITE?

You are expected to write two folio pieces of 1000 words each, which will account for 30% of your final grade. For people who are not always at their best in exams, this is a chance to make a major difference to your grade.

WHAT ARE MY CHOICES?

One of your two pieces will be drawn from the genres identified in Group A, the other from Group B. The group possibilities are as follows:

Group A: Creative

- a personal/reflective essay
- a piece of prose fiction (e.g. short story, episode from a novel)
- a poem or set of thematically linked poems
- a dramatic script (e.g. scene, monologue, sketch)

Group B: Discursive

- a piece of transactional writing
- a persuasive essay
- an argumentative essay
- a report for a specified purpose

Before making any decisions about your choices, let's take a look at two popular genres in each group to see what each one involves. That way, you'll have a better idea which ones best match up to your skills.

Group A: Creative

Prose fiction	Personal/reflective
If you are someone who has always enjoyed writing short stories or episodes from a novel, this is a really pleasurable choice. If you are not already sure if this is something you enjoy, a folio piece for an important exam probably isn't the best place to find out.	Nobody can write better about you or your life than you yourself. You already have all the information to hand, it's just a question of digging deep to bring the experience alive for others.
Opportunities Within the word limit, you are free to create your own world. Here you are free to conjure up atmospheric settings, characters who become convincingly alive, dialogue that fully reflects the characters and their lifestyles. Their fates are all in your gift. You must be prepared to explore all the possibilities of figurative language in the way of a professional writer.	**Opportunities** This needs to have all the same power to create setting, characters and dialogue as a short story. The difference is that you are not creating an imaginary world, it's one in which you have lived yourself. You will need to have the same ability to establish atmosphere in the way of the short-story writer. The only difference is that your narrative is true and anchored in reality.
Considerations A successful piece of short fiction needs a strong sense of structure, it cannot just ramble on. You will find the word limit imposes restrictions on any unnecessary introductions. Here a plan is very necessary before you begin. Feel free to alter it, but never lose sight of the overall shape. Limit your characters if they are to be described fully. Remember that contrasting characters will spark conflict which is great for moving stories on.	**Considerations** You need to choose your material really well. It must have sufficient depth for you to reflect on it and on any lessons it taught you. Discovering you had a talent you had not previously suspected will provide this depth; a day out to a safari park probably will not. Reflecting on some incident from your past could allow you to discuss how time has given you a new perspective on the event/experience.

contd

Group B: Discursive

Argumentative/persuasive	Transactional
If you feel that imaginative writing is not your strong point, but you have a strong interest in a topic, enjoy researching for information, organising your findings in a convincing way and presenting them with authority, then this might be a sensible choice for you.	Transactional writing is about getting things done when a written document can achieve this. If you are a practical person, this choice might suit you very well. It may take the form of a report, a review, a brochure, a memorandum, a letter or whatever format is appropriate for your task in hand.
Opportunities Here you can explore your chosen topic in two ways: you can try to persuade others to share your viewpoint on an issue; you can debate two sides of topic by laying out the facts of a case in a logically organised structure. The essential is to enjoy researching and sharing your results in prose which reads fluently and carries real conviction.	**Opportunities** This kind of writing is the kind which you can usefully carry over into the world of work, since it requires a 'real-world' mindset to be successful. You are attempting to convey information in a way that will assist the reader to understand the realities and practicalities of a situation. Your prose needs to guide the reader clearly through factual material of various kinds.
Considerations Getting the tone correct for whatever discursive option you select is of key importance here. Persuasive writing requires you to adopt an outgoing, emotive approach; argumentative debating or factual report-writing require you to adopt a much more neutral tone. Which of these approaches best suits you? Remember, too, the best discursive writing needs research to convince, but facts cannot be allowed to substitute clearly presented viewpoints of your own.	**Considerations** Your information needs to be as carefully researched as it would be in a persuasive or argumentative essay. Since practical considerations are also concerned, for example the transmission of information, the sequencing of actions, the timing of events, the communication of instructions, there can be no overlooking of factual detail vital to the successful completion of the task. Your prose needs to be totally at the service of the information to be communicated.

THINGS TO DO AND THINK ABOUT

Notice that we have not looked at all the genres you might explore in your folio. Remember, however, that the writing of poetry and plays is a highly specialised art. Perhaps you have experience of writing in these genres and have had your work noticed by experts in these fields. If this is the case, then these might be choices worth considering. For most candidates, however, the possibilities we have looked at above are probably the most accessible and offer choices with which you will perhaps feel most comfortable – and which offer you the surest chances of success.

ONLINE

For some advice about writing short stories, visit 'Your Story Club: How to write short stories – 10 tips with examples by our chief editor' at www.brightredbooks.net/N5Engish

ONLINE TEST

Check if you have chosen the best writing option online at www.brightredbooks.net/N5English

DON'T FORGET

Don't finally commit yourself to any essay choice until you are sure you know enough about the topic or are really keen to learn about it.

DON'T FORGET

Start to try out ideas and plans well before the deadline; be prepared to accept that your first thoughts might not be your best ones. Successful folio-writing is about being willing to draft and redraft several times before you even think of presenting a first version to your teacher.

WRITING CREATIVELY

ONLINE

Use this online guide to the elements in a short story for extra help in getting started: 'Short story elements' at www.brightredbooks.net/N5English

WRITING PROSE FICTION

Short story or episode from a novel? An intriguing choice – but, whichever you choose, remember that **character** and **setting** are as important as **plot** in both. Characters that do not come alive, who simply remain names on a page, fail to engage the reader's interest; narratives that take place in a vacuum create little in the way of atmosphere to catch the reader's attention. Remember, too, that your word limit is only 1000 words. That means you have to set certain limitations on your narrative. Keep this in mind when you set about your planning.

So, how do you go about planning your prose fiction?

One way is to set yourself a number of 'wh-' tasks which you can tackle in any order you wish, depending on how you like to compose fiction. Do you prefer starting with setting, characters or plot? Here are some starting points.

Where?	• Setting is a key factor in a good short story. A detailed, realistic setting is a grand start to a fiction piece. But don't do it well in the first paragraphs and then forget all about it. Keep it going with brief references to it as the story progresses.
	• To write well about setting, you need to know it intimately. Write from your knowledge, either first-hand or from research.
	• Given your word limit, restrict changing setting too often. You will use up too many words.
	• Think of films you have enjoyed where the setting transported you to somewhere that felt totally real. Your narrative should do the same.
Who?	• Your word limit means you would do well to restrict your characters to a number you can describe adequately. Don't introduce characters who play little part in the final outcome. Two, three or four might be a sensible cast list.
	• Contrasting characters often lead to conflict, which moves a story along very nicely. For example, try contrasting youth and age, rich and poor, sensible and rash, shy and outspoken or good-natured and quick-tempered.
	• Jot down facts about each character before you start. Not just appearance, but personality traits, nervous habits, likes, dislikes, hobbies, interests, tastes in music, people, food and so on. Don't blurt these all out at once, but weave them from time to time into your narrative. Passing references to such features bring characters alive.
What?	• Again, your word limit reduces the kind of story you can handle here. Epic adventures are out. To be successful, a good short narrative need not be about dramatic events; a minor incident carefully observed and imaginatively related is more likely to suit the required length of your text. Time sequences of hours, days or weeks are probably more practical than years or decades as your time frame.
When?	• The present causes less trouble, but if you have an interest in earlier periods, some basic research might furnish a credibly different setting, while a fertile imagination could provide the detail necessary to convince in a sci-fi tale.
	• Remember that setting encompasses not only a place and period but the seasons, weather and time of day as well. These can be manipulated tellingly to bring atmospheric colour to your fiction. Use them to reflect changing moods and attitudes of your characters in their situations. For example, spring/green shoots/hope or evening/mist/threat.
Why?	• Credibility is something you need to be alert to. So, why something happens needs to be addressed carefully. The far-fetched can weaken even the most carefully realised settings and characters. Keep the plot within the bounds of the believable.
How?	• As important as the 'wh-' questions is the question of how the story is to be told. Is the narrator to be 'I'? This will bring you close to the speaker and his/her thoughts. Or are you going to use the third-person narrator: he or she? This will let you observe everyone and allow you into everyone's thought processes.
	• And how is the plot to advance? In normal time sequence or by a dramatic flash-forward or flash-back? These latter two will get you off to a flying start before you go back and fill in the details. Many successful films use this technique.

A USEFUL STRUCTURE FOR A PLOT

Some guides to writing short stories will tell you that the following is a useful structure:

- A settled situation involving a minimum of characters (perhaps two or three).

- A complication deriving from something happening: a letter arriving, an accident, a new character appearing, the loss of someone or something.

- An increase in tension due to the new situation.

- A crisis leading to a turning point in the affairs of all concerned.

- An ending with a perceived change in matters compared with how they stood at the start. Perhaps the unhappy are now happier, perhaps a relationship has altered – for the better or the worse, or perhaps characters simply have changed their view on themselves or someone else. Or perhaps we readers have changed our perception of a character or situation.

You can probably think of many good short stories which use only some of these features or perhaps none at all. But, if you are stuck for a structure, this might be a useful starting point.

THINGS TO DO AND THINK ABOUT

As a starting point for your study of short stories, try *Hieroglyphics and Other Stories* by Anne Donovan. Donovan is a master at taking the events of everyday life and arousing our interest in and sympathy for the characters involved, while furnishing wonderfully varied settings. Watch out for her use of metaphors, similes and symbols and learn how they can be used to give impact to situations.

✔ ONLINE TEST

Test the strength of your plot against this online checklist: www. brightredbooks.net/N5English

✛ DON'T FORGET

Of course, the best way to learn to write convincing short stories is to read as many of them as you can! Your school or college library will have no shortage of anthologies. Try looking out for the *Oxford Book of Scottish Short Stories* or the *Oxford Book of Short Stories*. They are both a rich mine of short story-writing from which you can learn a lot.

EXAMINING FICTION FOR WRITING TIPS

Early on in this section, we suggested that many of the techniques you learned about in Close Reading or in analysing fiction could help you with your writing. How? Well, when analysing how writers make certain effects, you frequently point out the use of short or minor sentences, inversion, imagery, word choice and suchlike techniques. So, once you have decided on your plan, think carefully about how the story is to be told. Think about using the techniques employed by professional writers in a story you've enjoyed to do tasks such as launching a narrative, establishing a setting or creating a character.

LAUNCHING A NARRATIVE

Here is the beginning of 'A Chitterin Bite' by Anne Donovan. Look at the techniques employed to capture the reader's attention right from the very start. Many are familiar to you from your Close Reading work.

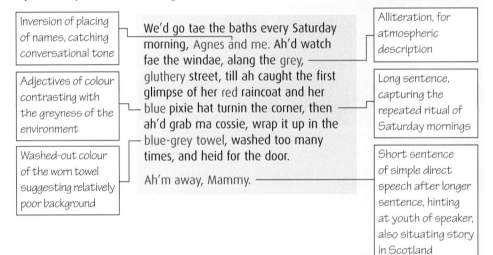

Inversion of placing of names, catching conversational tone

Adjectives of colour contrasting with the greyness of the environment

Washed-out colour of the worn towel suggesting relatively poor background

We'd go tae the baths every Saturday morning, Agnes and me. Ah'd watch fae the windae, alang the grey, gluthery street, till ah caught the first glimpse of her red raincoat and her blue pixie hat turnin the corner, then ah'd grab ma cossie, wrap it up in the blue-grey towel, washed too many times, and heid for the door.

Ah'm away, Mammy.

Alliteration, for atmospheric description

Long sentence, capturing the repeated ritual of Saturday mornings

Short sentence of simple direct speech after longer sentence, hinting at youth of speaker, also situating story in Scotland

Here, in only around 100 words, Anne Donovan has used some techniques with which you are familiar to do various things: to create, with great economy, a social setting for the two girls; to establish the fact of their ongoing friendship; to give an idea of their age. Nothing has been spelt out, but all the information is there. Note, too, Donovan's use of Scots for both narrative and dialogue, which further positions her characters. Scots for either narrative or dialogue might give an added sense of realism to your writing, too, depending on the situation you are creating.

LET'S LOOK AT THAT

Here is someone trying to use similar techniques to create a story of his own. Note there is no slavish attempt to mimic exactly Donovan's writing, but lessons have been learned.

> *Inversion of placing of names, catching conversational tone*

> *Short burst of direct speech to contrast with this sentence and signal age, Scottish origin and sporting interests of speaker*

We were inseparable in those days, Watty and me. And the Monday-night routine was always the same: Watty would arrive on his silver-sprayed sports bike with the Wonder-Woman transfers, dump it any-old-how behind our straggly hedge, bang on the door since the bell had long since given up the ghost – and dad had never been a great DIY fan.

Training's finishing late, dad. See ya.

> *Alliteration to bring alive the garish quality of the bike*

> *Long sentence to catch the routine nature of the Monday-night ritual and nature of family*

And here, as you can see, alertness to the techniques learned in analysing text can bring alive your own writing. Don't let your knowledge of inversion, the contrasting of long and short sentences, alliteration, imagery – and all the other techniques you have learned – remain shut away in your Close Reading knowledge. You shouldn't follow a model from a professional writer slavishly, but be aware of possibilities. Apply aspects of them thoughtfully to your own writing where you think they will add interest. Experiment with them. They should make a difference to the colour and readability of what you write.

THINGS TO DO AND THINK ABOUT

Before you start out on a full-scale narrative, try out a few small-scale practice pieces to establish setting. It's a bit like a painter trying a few sketches before starting on a full-scale oil painting. Here are two brief situations which you might treat as the openings of a narrative.

Your task here is to create a convincing setting, using perhaps some of the following: onomatopoeia, imagery, alliteration, assonance, inversion or a variety of short and long sentences. Use any other techniques you think useful.

1 *It is a moonlit, frosty December night around ten o'clock. This character is entering a wooded area which he/she needs to cross to get home after a night out with friends. Bring the setting alive for the reader. Think of including the character's feelings if you can.*

2 *You wake up in a hotel room in some holiday destination, having arrived late at night. You have not seen much of the surroundings. The sun wakens you. You get up, open the blinds. Describe what you see and feel.*

How well did your writing go? Get a partner to underline any techniques he/she saw at work. Get their comment on how convincing your setting was. Do they have anything to add? This was just for practice – but, if it went well, could you develop one of these openings for the start of your real story?

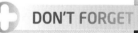

CREATING CONVINCING CHARACTERS

THE SURFACE AND BENEATH

Happily, there is no single way of bringing characters alive on the page. Describing **appearance** is of course a start.

EXAMPLE:

Here is Ian Rankin describing Ludovic Lumsden in *Black & Blue*. Much of the detail goes into the description of his clothes; but, towards the end, lifestyle details creep in:

> Lumsden wore a blue blazer with shiny brass buttons, grey trousers, black slip-on shoes. His shirt was an elegant blue and white stripe, his tie salmon-pink. The clothes made him look like the secretary of some exclusive club, but the face and body told another story. He was six feet two, wiry, with cropped fair hair emphasising a widow's peak. His eyes weren't so much red-rimmed as chlorinated, the irises a piercing blue. No wedding ring. He could have been anywhere between thirty and forty years old. (p. 166)

Lumsden comes across as a smart dresser, but his obvious keenness for keeping fit is also suggested. He will turn out to be a corrupt policeman, but at the moment Rankin's depiction is neutral. Or is he just *too* smart to be true?

EXAMPLE:

Louise Welsh in 'The Cutting Room' adopts a very different approach to character presentation. Here the description is not in the objective third person but in a very subjective first-person narrative where we learn much more about Rilke, a Glasgow auctioneer, than simply his appearance:

> I'm twenty-five years at the auction house, forty-three years of age. They call me Rilke to my face, behind my back, the Cadaver, Corpse, Walking Dead. Aye, well, I may be gaunt of face and long of limb but I don't smell and I never expect anything. (p. 2)

Physical description is kept brief here (*gaunt of face and long of limb* – which, of course, we know from our Close Reading work is an example of a parallel structure), but we also learn something of his **personality**: shrewdly knowledgeable about how he is viewed by others behind his back and yet chattily accepting of their nastiness (*Aye, well, I may be ... but I don't smell and I never expect anything*).

Let's try that out!

Using the approach adopted by Rankin and the approach adopted by Welsh, construct two descriptions of yourself as if you were a character in a short story. In the first, catch your physical appearance; in the second, try to hint at your personality, too. Go back and look at sentence structure in both, use of imagery, informal tone, narrative stance (third person and first person), parallel structures; try to incorporate what you think useful into your own writing here.

ONLINE

For more great character entrances, check out this article: '13 Great Movie Character Entrances' at www.brightredbooks.net/ N5English

SHOW, DON'T TELL

Think about the entrance of Tybalt in the Baz Luhrmann film of *Romeo and Juliet*. He exits his car, grinding a cigarette butt under his metal heel in a way that suggests his cruelty and aggression long before he says anything. Think of other films where a small action can reveal much about character and mood: a flower placed carefully on a breakfast tray, a beer-can crushed in a fist. Make small, giveaway actions part of your equipment for tackling character creation.

contd

Let's try that out!

Thinking of how actions can establish character, work with a partner on inventing actions you could integrate into your narrative to signal in advance to readers the characters of the following people:

an impatient person, a generous person, a hostile person,
a nervous person, a person with something to hide

Now try to write a sentence or two on each one, integrating this selected action into the launch of their character.

> **EXAMPLE:**
>
> A clumsy person
>
> > Entering in some haste, Jackson's left foot caught the cable of my desk-lamp, bringing it crashing to the floor at his feet. 'Sorry. This is always happening to me,' he said, looking up apologetically as he bent to pick up the smashed, smoking bulb.
>
> Here we're shown, not told, that Jackson is clumsy. How much more effective is this than the comment: *Jackson is the clumsiest person I know*?

Could short extracts like this perhaps trigger ideas for a short story? How might the speaker react to Jackson here? Who precisely is Jackson, and why is he here? Short bursts of writing in this way can sometimes lead to unexpected bonuses. Try it.

YOU ARE WHAT YOU SPEAK

If actions can help to create characters, so too can speech habits. The type of **dialogue** you give to your characters can also spare you a lot of explanatory writing. Here your knowledge of sentence structure should help you a lot. Characters can come alive by the way they talk.

Let's try that out!

In the grid below on the left, you will see a variety of speech habits at work. Match them with their character-type suggested by the column on the right.

It's a job where ... how shall I put it? ... Where you need, you know ... to be, well, just a bit ... a bit ... decisive. Mm ... Yes, quite ... decisive.	**BOSSY**
Fetch me the television guide. And bring my glasses. Not the old ones. And put the cat out since you're up. Hop to it, sunshine!	**INSECURE**
Does this really suit me? Am I maybe too old to be wearing rugby shirts? Is it not just a bit flash? Or am I just being a bit neurotic here? What do you think?	**BORING**
I've been secretary of this bowling club now for many more years than I care to remember, more years than you've been alive I'd say, but I've always enjoyed the work, the excitement of the tournaments, the many generations of bowlers who've come my way, grand folk, all of them.	**BRISK**
Now, then. Let's see. Jake, you alright taking the girls? I'll follow in the Range Rover. Shall we meet up in Carlisle? It'll take about an hour. Right. Off we go!	**VAGUE**

Here we see that vague people may tend to leave sentences incomplete or fragmented; bossy ones may fire off a series of commands; insecure ones perhaps favour a series of questions seeking reassurance; long-winded, boring people might go in for rather lengthy sentences; and brisk, dynamic ones may express themselves in a series of short sentences.

THINGS TO DO AND THINK ABOUT

Appearance, actions, speech habits, mannerisms, taste in clothes, music, films, nervous tics: they all play their part in humanising your characters. And the features that make up their characters need to crop up throughout the tale, not be confined to some opening statements.

DON'T FORGET

Having a cast list composed of a mixture of Scots and English speakers could provide you with a rich, contrasting texture of languages. Or perhaps try having a character who may switch from one to the other for various reasons? Think about how that might be useful.

ONLINE TEST

See if you can recognise more characteristics through descriptions, actions and speech online at www.brightredbooks.net/N5English

DON'T FORGET

Watch out for all the possibilities for establishing a character by using *other* characters to comment on the individual you are trying to create. Imagine, say, an unpleasant character, infuriated by the good works of a decent one, speaking hostilely of her/him. That tells us a lot about *both* characters.

PERSONAL REFLECTIVE WRITING

Let's get one thing straight: personal reflective writing is **not** creative writing. It needs, however, to present the reader with an experience that is just as rich and rewarding as reading a short story or novel. The difference is that the events and experiences described are true and taken from your own life.

The reflection which emerges derives from these events and experience. This reflection is there to demonstrate that you are capable of viewing biographical material in a way that presents you as a thoughtful person, one who sees significance in what has been experienced and perhaps learned.

ONLINE

Read this article about the best college applications in the USA, most of which come from everyday experiences in personal reflective writing: 'The *New York Times*: Some of the more mundane moments in life make great essays' at www. brightredbooks.net/N5English

BUT NOTHING EVER HAPPENS TO ME!

No, you probably haven't won an Olympic medal or been an *X-Factor* finalist, but successful personal reflective writing doesn't really rely on news-making experiences of this kind. Success in personal reflective writing can stem from very ordinary everyday experiences or events which, when explored in some detail, reveal that there is a lot more to you and your life than you think. Here are just a few ways of exploring that life.

ME, MYSELF AND I

There are so many angles to your life that the problem might be knowing where to start. Asking yourself a series of questions might help you to sort out a starting point.

Who am I?

This might seem rather an obvious place to start, but think about it for a moment. You would first need to consider yourself in your own assessment, but how do your friends, family or teachers appear to regard you? Are you the person they think you are, or is there another 'you', one you would like them to see? Or is there another 'you' who you'd like to be? How do you intend to bridge this gap? Talking about incidents or conversations which illustrate these various viewpoints would occupy several sections, with a final section bringing together your verdict on how you view the way forward.

Examining yourself from yet another angle, you might wish to write about your present personality when compared with the person you used to be when younger. How have you changed? What brought about these changes? How do you feel about these changes? Exploring precise events or incidents that might have triggered these changes could be highly productive.

What do I do?

The way you pass your time when you are not committed to the educational process can be dissected in many different ways. Obviously, there are leisure activities and hobbies which help to make you the person you are. How you first became aware of this activity, your first reactions to it, key incidents along the way, how you have changed as a person or what you have gained or learned as a result of the exposure to it are just some of the things that might be included.

For those with employment after or before school or college hours, the possibilities are equally rich in potential. A need for additional financial resources probably drove you to seek employment in the first place, but what were your feelings about this? What did

contd

you learn as you set about looking for work; how did you react to any upsets along the way? Working with other people poses certain challenges; were there episodes where you learned that the workplace can be very different from your educational experience? Using key incidents, illustrate what you have experienced, gained or learned about yourself, people and life generally.

Who do I care about?

Relationships of all kinds are central to everyone's life. And relationships change as time passes. Families break up and reform in other ways. Weddings and funerals affect us with many different, sometimes conflicting, emotions. Relationships within families alter as we grow up and develop. The same is equally true of solid friendships formed in early years, which we see changing as the years pass. Are there key moments or incidents which brought about these alterations? Describing these key incidents or events and exploring your feelings as they occurred can help you to come to terms with them. And comparing them with your feelings today is an exercise which offers rich pickings for personal reflective work.

What have I learned?

As we grow and develop, life can deal us all kinds of knocks and bruises. All experience, however, is surely useful for what it teaches us about ourselves and life in general. Failure can sometimes be more instructive than success. Examining disappointment can be a really therapeutic and constructive activity. On the other hand, sometimes we are taught about life without any painful experience at all, through encountering people who have inspired us or taught us a lot about life without setting out to do so. Watching a friend or family member deal with a difficult situation might teach us about courage, determination or loyalty. The incidents and people from whom we learn offer material to describe and reflect on in depth.

THINGS TO DO AND THINK ABOUT

With a partner or in a group, look at the questions above from the viewpoint of your own experience and extract two or three possibilities which might form the starting point for an essay of this kind. Discuss frankly with the group what you might include, and see how others respond to your choices. The experiences/incidents might be interesting, but what have they to say about their usefulness in offering sufficient depth for reflection? Check with your partner(s).

ONLINE TEST

Test your idea for a personal reflective piece against this checklist online: www.brightredpublishing.net/N5English

DON'T FORGET

A politician once commented:

I was brought up to believe that how I saw myself was more important than how others saw me.

Robert Burns rather turned this on its head when he said:

> *O, wad some Power the giftie gie us To see oursels as others see us!*

Irrespective which of these remarks you believe to be more in tune with your thinking, keep both in mind as you write. Reflection on how you see yourself and how others may be viewing you will only add depth and breadth to your material.

PERSONAL REFLECTIVE WRITING (CONTD)

CAN PUBLISHED AUTHORS HELP HERE?

As we said earlier, personal reflective writing is derived from your lived experience. But some of the techniques of fiction-writing can be useful in recreating this reality for others. If outsiders are to understand the events and experiences described, your writing needs to bring your experiences and feelings alive. Your use of words must help others to see and feel exactly what you felt. So, once again, figurative language, sentence structure, alliteration, word choice and all the other techniques you know about need to be harnessed with all the skill of a professional writer to bring about this end.

Here is noted Scottish writer Kathleen Jamie sharing personal experience in an episode when she discovered her interest in archaeology by taking part in a 'dig' on leaving school:

> *Then, one day in May 1979, it may even have been my seventeenth birthday, I sat my last, lacklustre exam and left school without ceremony or much notion of a personal failure. A day or two later, my mother drove me the thirty miles from our house into rural Perthshire. She had suggested librarianship, which was the stock idea for a kid who read books. I did read books: the paperback stuffed into my haversack on the back seat was by Tom Wolfe – 'The Electric Kool-Aid Acid Test'. She suggested secretarial college. When she said these things, tears of belligerent dismay pricked at my eyes. No one suggested university.*

Consoling her was her first taste of the life of archaeological fieldwork:

> *We worked by day, but the long midsummer evenings were our own; we were free to linger outdoors in the cool gloamings, at leisure until work began again in the morning. About twenty of us dossed down in the farmhouse at night, and every morning we filed out onto site. I loved it.*

> (from Kathleen Jamie, 'The Woman in the Field', in *Sightlines*, Sort Of Books, 2012)

Let's try that out!

Either on your own or with a partner, go over these extracts to discover by what means Jamie brought this experience alive for those of us not present. Look also to see how she presented her reactions and feelings as the narrative advances. Keep these in mind when you start to write.

PRE-WRITING REFLECTION

You are by now well aware of the need for considered reflection stemming from the events and experiences you are about to describe. But before you even begin think about your plan – whatever form it may take – you need to reflect on which aspects of your material you are confident will add *relevantly* to the situation you are about to discuss. All kinds of remembered detail will pop into your head, but you will not have space for all of them. Decide which ones *really* are relevant to your overall view of what you want to say. Not everything you remember will add focus to your narrative.

Your pre-writing reflection will also need to consider which parts of the experience or events you *really* remember in detail of the kind that might interest the reader.

Only once you have dealt with this can you get down to your plan.

PLANNING FOR REFLECTIVE WRITING

Just as a piece of creative writing needs some structuring shape to give it interest, so too does personal reflective writing. The section above entitled 'Me, myself and I' makes some suggestions as to areas you may wish to include in your plan, but each plan will require its own structure to be dictated by what it is setting out to do and say.

If, for example, you are embarking on the description of some important event – sporting, family or musical, say – don't overlook the usefulness of the weather that day (did it match your mood or not?); the behaviour of those around you (did they seem to be supportive or otherwise?); the venue itself (did it intimidate you or did you find it exciting?); or mood swings you noticed in yourself or others. These are details which, handled with due regard for the techniques we mentioned earlier, will create a vivid picture for the reader.

If, on the other hand, you are going to discuss an activity or person that altered your life in some way, you will need to fill in background details of when contact first happened, your initial responses, your developing reactions, key incidents along the way, the changes noted in your life and so on.

Whatever your choice of personal reflective subject, it would be wise to ensure that you have not only allowed space for final reflection in the closing paragraphs but also managed to integrate reflective observations into the narrative as it goes along – as, indeed, did Kathleen Jamie in the extract earlier.

WHY IS REFLECTION IMPORTANT?

No matter how exciting and lively your narrative, you must be sure that you have combined it with the kind of reflection that establishes you as a thinking person, one honest enough to admit to weaknesses (where they exist) but also sufficiently confident to claim development in your personality or view of the world.

There has to be a balance between convincingly narrated experience and the kind of thoughtfulness that suggests you have interpreted this material with maturing reflection. You may find that this type of reflection is not only a persuasive way to complete this folio assignment but also a powerful way of understanding developments in yourself and those around you.

ONLINE

For more tips on how to plan and execute a great piece of personal reflective writing, read this article: 'How to write an effective reflective essay' at www. brightredbooks.net/N5English

DON'T FORGET

Reflection does not need to wait until the closing stages of your essay. It is sensible to build it into your advancing narrative, too.

THINGS TO DO AND THINK ABOUT

A practice exercise before you begin your essay might be to find a photograph in which you figure with a few friends, say at a picnic or outing. Describe the event, the time, the weather and the place where this was taken. Think, too, about your relations with the others in the photograph – what they were then and what they are now. How do you feel about yourself at that time? There you are! You have started personal reflective writing!

WRITING DISCURSIVELY

In this group, you have a choice between writing an argumentative essay or a persuasive one. So, what are the differences?

- An argumentative essay is one in which you explore and evaluate opposing viewpoints on a controversial topic in formal and strictly neutral language, calling on objective data before offering any final opinion of your own.

- A persuasive essay is one in which you attempt to win over the reader to your view on a controversial topic. Here, too, there will be researched data to substantiate your viewpoint, but it will not be similarly balanced as in an argumentative essay. Contrary viewpoints may be entertained but only to be dismissed. Here the language will be unashamedly emotive as it seeks reader approval.

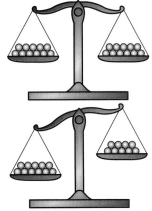

These are very different approaches to a topic, as you can see. But there are also likenesses, too, likenesses which it might be helpful to consider before making a final choice of one or the other.

ONLINE

If your topic reflects current issues and debates, the chances are that published texts may not have caught up with them fully yet. Quality journals and newspapers can help greatly here. Using a search engine, tap in your topic or issue followed by a quality online newspaper of your choice (the *Independent*, the *Guardian*, the *Herald*, the *Scotsman*, for example) to see what is available.

ARGUMENTATIVE AND PERSUASIVE: FAMILY LIKENESSES

Whichever approach you decide on, your completed essay must offer the reader just as much satisfaction on completion as any piece of fiction or reflective writing. So, how is this sense of satisfaction achieved? Let's answer this by asking some of the questions your reader might be asking of your argumentative or persuasive essay.

Why is this subject worthy of attention? In your introduction to an essay of either approach, you must establish enough background information to convince the reader that the topic is sufficiently important and compelling to be worth reading about, particularly if it is not currently in the news.

Is the writer respecting the genre? It would be foolish to set out to write an argumentative essay and then slip into personal views along the way, thus destroying your claim to objectivity. It would be similarly foolish for the writer of a persuasive essay to end up simply presenting information rather than seeking to persuade.

How reliable is the research? Your sources should be acknowledged at the end of your essay. So, how well will your list read? Nutritional 'facts' from the website of a fast-food manufacturer could hardly be taken to be evidence of sound research. Website information might be useful as a starting point for topics which have only recently touched our consciousness. So far, these may not have been dealt with in book form, but more traditional topics will have been explored in peer-reviewed publications. These are usually the most reliable and authoritative. Quality journals and newspapers employ acknowledged experts and pollsters whose accuracy and readability can usually be counted on. These, of course, can be viewed online, mostly free of charge. A list of sources balanced between the paper-based and the electronic will impress.

How up-to-date is the information? In this multimedia age of 24-hour newsgathering, there is no excuse for outdated statistics and information. Check publication dates of books, journals and newspapers and posting dates of websites before beginning note-taking.

Have sections been plagiarised? Research means note-taking. While engaged in this, ensure that you do not 'lift' unacknowledged stretches of text. Lifting text from website or publications is simply theft, and experienced examiners have a sixth sense

contd

for detecting it. Often, this 'lifting' may have been accidental, but you must be alive to the danger. To avoid this, as you take notes, use a highlighter to differentiate quotations from your own notes, paying attention to the details of the author's name and status, place of publication and date of extract. Another way to avoid the dangers of inadvertent plagiarism is to put the idea straight into your own words, while, again, acknowledging whose idea this originally was.

ONLINE

Check out the 'International debate education association' at www.brightredbooks. net/N5English. Tap on the *Debatabase* strapline at the top of the Home page, and you will find 14 headings such as Education, Health, Politics, Society, Sport, Science, International and so on, under which are dozens of associated debates with arguments for and against which are well articulated. Check out if there are bibliographic references at the end of each contribution to ensure that there is authoritative backing for the points made. The Point/ Counterpoint format makes it particularly helpful for argumentative essays, although its enormous database of facts makes this site equally useful for persuasive writing, too.

THE NEED FOR AUTHORITY

Just as you need evidence in your critical essay, so, too, do you need it in discursive writing. Whether you decide on an argumentative essay or a persuasive one, you need evidence to support your case. In a critical essay, this took the form of close reference to the text or a quotation. Here it is the backing of what we call authority. By this, we mean the opinion of an acknowledged expert in their field, the results of a respected poll or a reference to a published study or report. In every instance, you need to make clear who your authority is, where and when the evidence appeared. Without authority, you are attempting to make out a case simply from your own subjective opinions. These, while no doubt interesting, will not carry the weight that expert opinion will. Having some expert evidence on both sides will immeasurably strengthen your arguments. But do not overuse this; it is only there to support *your* case.

ONLINE TEST

Test your idea for a discursive writing piece and your proposed research methods online at www. brightredbooks.net/N5English

THINGS TO DO AND THINK ABOUT

Argumentative and persuasive essays, for all their differences, share many characteristics. They both may contain:

- illustrative examples or anecdotes: to aid readers' understanding

- expert opinion: to support or criticise a point of view

- analogies: to suggest parallels with other situations to aid understanding

- polls or survey results: to demonstrate research-backed evidence

- warnings: to indicate ability to follow through implications of findings.

How they each use these shared features is, of course, very different, as we shall see later.

DON'T FORGET

You will never be penalised for opinions which run counter to those of the examiner. You are being assessed on the strength of your argued case, not the nature of your beliefs.

WRITING ARGUMENTATIVELY

LAUNCHING THE ARGUMENTATIVE STRUCTURE

In a successful argumentative essay, writers take a controversial topic and conduct in-depth research before presenting data to support both sides of the argument. Finally, if they so choose, they may award support to one viewpoint or the other. Balance of factual presentation and neutrality of language are the hallmarks of this form of essay.

The opening paragraph is particularly important for establishing your credentials as a reliable investigator of the topic. It needs to suggest that you are reliably informed, clear-sighted in your appraisal of the opposing viewpoints and well organised in your presentation of material. Let's see how an introduction for this kind of essay might work.

A topic that has aroused much controversy is fracking. This is a relatively new means of obtaining oil and gas which has environmentalists and businesspeople at loggerheads with each other. After studying the pros and cons of the topic, we might come up with the following format for the introduction:

Title in itself balances both viewpoints. Note the order in which they appear.	**Fracking: false prophet or real profit?**
Significance of topic established in first two sentences.	*The world is fast running out of polluting fossil fuels. Renewable sources of clean energy such as wind and solar power as yet seem some way from offering reliable alternatives. According to some experts, hydraulic fracturing, or fracking, is a plausible alternative to both. But what actually is it? Put simply, it is a process which extracts natural gas and oil from rock formations deep underground by fracturing and injecting chemicals into them. Opponents claim it is a dangerous tampering with nature, one which risks polluting water supplies and even causing earth tremors. Supporters claim it offers Britain a profitable source of secure energy which reduces exposure to international political upheavals. What exactly are the associated dangers, and how exactly could fracking help our environmentally concerned world?*
Topic defined in third, fourth and fifth sentences	
Sentence six sets out one side of argument – the negative.	
Sentence seven sets out the positive viewpoint.	
Sentence eight suggests how the essay will develop (a) by examining the dangers and (b) by investigating the benefits. A road-map.	

Notice that in the title, in the setting out of the two arguments and in the final sentence, the positive is mentioned last, hinting perhaps on what side the essay will finally come down.

ORDERING YOUR ARGUMENTS

Like a critical essay, an argumentative essay should present a flow of ideas which carries readers comfortably along, with no sudden or unexplained changes of direction to jar or puzzle them. The sensible ordering of your ideas and arguments will strengthen your case-making skills immeasurably in the eyes of the examiner. So, how will you ensure this seamless flow of text?

One way would be to examine your evidence and then decide where your final verdict falls: are you for or against an idea? Suppose you decided you were **for** fracking as discussed earlier. Then you might usefully consider the following order of presentation:

- An introduction which sets out both sides but places the positive second
- Subsequent paragraphs/sections which deal with the hazards of fracking
- Leading to paragraphs/section looking at fracking's benefits
- A summative conclusion making finally clear where you stand on fracking, i.e. in favour of it.

Why this particular order?

Well, suppose you were in favour of fracking but left discussing its dangers until the second half of your essay. Consider, then, the effect on your readers if, in the very next, concluding paragraph, you abruptly announced that you were in favour of a process that you had just been expertly criticising. This can puzzle and disconcert your readers: one minute you are pointing out the shortcomings of an issue, the next you are saying you are in favour of it.

If you are in favour of a topic, then banish a discussion of its negative points to earlier in the essay so that your positive case seamlessly precedes your positive conclusion. The reader will not have forgotten your negative points, but the positive ones will be fresher in his/her mind, and your approval of them will seem all the more understandable and logical.

The reverse also holds good: if you are against an issue, acknowledge its benefits first and then discuss its shortcomings so as to lead into a conclusion that follows naturally on from these shortcomings.

If you decide to withhold an opinion of your own, be careful how you do so. This is a perfectly legitimate position to take up, but make sure you give a reason: current lack of credible evidence, a rapidly changing situation, or perhaps ultimately a verdict will depend on the individual's political/social/cultural views. Make sure you have reasons for rejection of commitment to one side or the other. If you do not, you risk simply looking like a ditherer.

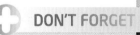

ONLINE TEST

Test your knowledge of what makes up a good argumentative essay online, at www.brightredbooks.net/N5English

ONLINE

Struggling for somewhere to start? See if any of the argumentative essay topics on this list inspire you: '50 argument essay topics' at www.brightredbooks.net/N5English

DON'T FORGET

When you are constructing a case in favour of an issue, begin with a point strong enough to gain credibility, then go on to a stronger one and then finish with your best one. In this way, your argument builds, getting stronger and more impressive as it advances.

THINGS TO DO AND THINK ABOUT

Are you perhaps unsure where you stand on an issue, even after you have conducted considerable research? Try this. Once you have collected your data, why not organise the points in 'for' and 'against' columns? Then try writing an introductory paragraph for **both** sides, in the style of our 'fracking' introduction. Which version are you more comfortable with? That may give you the pointer you are looking for.

WRITING PERSUASIVELY

THE LANGUAGE OF PERSUASION

This is a form of writing which responds well to strong opinions. These opinions need, however, to be credibly supported by researched data, otherwise your essay will sound like an empty rant. There are plenty of models out there for you to study. Try first of all looking in the 'Opinion', 'Comment' or 'Leader' pages of a quality newspaper. Or listen to a politician making a speech in parliament. Here you'll find plenty of tips for writing (and speaking) persuasively. You'll notice that authority is often cited but skilfully manipulated to back up personal points of view. So, what would you do well to consider including? Let's take a look at some possibilities.

Involvement of reader

The use of pronouns such as 'we' and 'you' see you absorbing the reader into your arguments. 'We suffer here from too much bureaucracy ...' Commands also bring the reader closer. 'Consider for a moment ...', 'Think how much better ...'

Emotive language

Emotionally loaded word choice will feature prominently, as it does in much media reporting. 'Families' may become 'hard-working families'; 'pensioners' may become 'cash-strapped pensioners'; a pregnant woman may become 'a heavily pregnant woman'. The aim is to arouse sympathy/support for or anger/criticism against people and issues in your chosen sphere of persuasive writing. If you cite authority figures, they will often have emotive phrases attached to their names: 'Was it not Sir Walter Scott, Scotland's greatest novelist, who claimed that ...?', or 'To quote the much-maligned Tim Henman: ...'

Rhetorical questions

These questions, to which no real answer is expected of the reader, figure prominently in articles, speeches and persuasive essays. (They may, however, sometimes be answered by writers themselves, for effect, to demonstrate their clever mastery of a seemingly difficult problem which he/she has brought to our attention.) The aim of their authors is to seek our support by appealing to our feelings. 'What kind of parent treats children in this way?' 'When will governments learn there is no support for such policies?' Used occasionally, particularly after a stretch of information in which emotive word choice has been well to the fore, the effect can be powerfully persuasive. Used too often, they tend to sound rather hollow.

Attitude markers

After some particularly informative yet emotive reporting of information, these can be useful in guiding reader response. 'Clearly then, ...', 'Obviously, ...', 'Surely, ...', 'Sadly, ...', 'Fortunately, ...' are just a few. Look out for opportunities to use them to win over readers to your committed stance.

Rising rhetorical triads

Don't be put off by their name. You have heard them many times in speeches you may have listened to. They figure prominently in writing that is meant to persuade. They are closely related to the persuasive devices of **repetition** and **parallel structures** about which you learned in Close Reading. These tripartite statements or phrases typically appear in the final section or paragraph, with each element gaining in strength as the writer seeks to build to a **climax**. 'This is a tramway system which will ... It is a system which will also ... It is a system which, above all, will ...'. Often they combine with rhetorical questions for even greater emotional impact. 'Is this the world we worked for? Is this the world we fought for? And is this a world worth passing on to our children?' Such a ringing close can work well in a persuasive essay, appealing as it does to the reader's emotional response. It will only work, however, if there is some solidly researched data elsewhere in the essay on which you can build such a final emotional pitch.

ONLINE

For more inspiration, check out the *Telegraph's* list of the 'Top 25 political speeches of all time' at www.brightredbooks.net/N5English

DON'T FORGET

The novelist Joseph Conrad once remarked:

'He who wants to persuade should put his trust not in the right argument, but in the right word. The power of sound has always been greater than the power of sense.'

With a partner or in a group, discuss whether you agree with Conrad. Do you see any dangers in this belief for you as a persuasive essay-writer?

ORDERING YOUR ARGUMENTS

In a persuasive essay, you are setting out to persuade readers of the rightness of your case. This frees you from the need to balance your arguments or present your case in language as neutral as in an argumentative essay. Here you are at liberty to use persuasive-language techniques of the kind we have just been discussing.

You must be careful, however, to marshal your arguments just as carefully as in an argumentative essay, although somewhat differently. To win over readers, it is wise to establish yourself as a sensible, reasonable person. And sensible, reasonable people are always aware that their opinion is not the only one around. How, then, do you deal with possibly contrary viewpoints when you set out to make your own persuasive case? As in an argumentative essay, it might be wise to deal with them early on in your essay so that your increasingly powerful arguments push them aside in the memory of your readers.

This might be a possible solution:

- An introduction in which you make your viewpoint abundantly clear.

- Acknowledge perhaps a conflicting opinion but refute it in a reasonable, logical way. It is always a good idea to show respect to contrary views.

- Launch your first persuasive paragraph.

- Continue with similarly persuasive paragraphs, saving your strongest argument until last.

- Conclusion.

ONLINE TEST

Check if your plan fits the bill online at www.brightredbooks.net/N5English

THINGS TO DO AND THINK ABOUT

Here is Ed Miliband in the closing section of his speech to his party conference in 2012. With a partner, list any persuasive devices you see at work here. Are there elements here that could be useful in the conclusion to your persuasive essay?

> Britain has given my family everything. Britain and the spirit, the determination, the courage of the people who rebuilt Britain after the Second World War. And now the question is asked again: who in this generation will rebuild Britain for the future? Who can come up to the task of rebuilding Britain? Friends, it falls to us, it falls to us, the Labour Party. As it has fallen to previous generations of Labour Party pioneers to leave our country a better place than we found it. Never to shrug our shoulders at injustice and say that is the way the world is. To come together, to join together, to work together as a country.
>
> It's not some impossible dream. We've heard it, we've seen it, we've felt it. That is my faith.

WRITING PERSUASIVELY (CONTD)

LAUNCHING THE PERSUASIVE STRUCTURE

As in an argumentative essay, you need to quickly establish yourself as an informed commentator yet one, this time, with a firmly committed point of view. Let's take a look at how we might organise that introduction to create the best possible effect. Here we might go back to the topic of fracking which we dealt with in our argumentative introduction.

Note title is unashamedly persuasive, using alliteration and a command to add impact.

First two sentences are questions which hook reader's attention by offering attractive propositions and also establish subject's significance.

Topic defined and explained in sentences three, four and five.

Attitude marker launches final sentence (a rhetorical question) which both lists benefits and signals structure sequence of essay.

Secure our future with fracking!

What would you say if we told you we were close to a source of fuel that was cheaper and potentially cleaner than oil and coal? What if we added that its extraction close to home would free us from the unpredictability of international politics? Hydraulic fracturing, or fracking, offers us hope on both fronts. But what actually is it? Put simply, it is a process which extracts natural gas and oil from rock formations deep underground by fracturing and injecting chemicals into them. Surely the time has come for all our politicians to get behind a process that offers enormous benefits to the environment, the economy and long-suffering consumers?

The writer in the introduction here is highly enthusiastic about the benefits of fracking. This is not the only view, of course. In the 'Things to Do and Think About' section at the end of this topic, there is the chance to explore the other side of the argument more fully.

STRUCTURING THE PERSUASIVE PARAGRAPH

Notice that the paragraphs in a persuasive essay, just as in a critical, argumentative or creative essay, can benefit from what is by now a familiar structure: a strong Statement (S) composed of one or more sentences to form the opening, followed by Evidence (E) whose significance is unpacked for us in a Commentary (C) of our own. Here are elements of a persuasive paragraph with that SEC structure:

For decades now, cosmetic surgery has bewitched yet bewildered women who feel their appearance falls far short of the image they crave. Research at the University of Geneva suggests that, in their desperate desire for change, women sometimes fail to make the most elementary of checks on … (STATEMENT) According to Professor Erica Martin, writing in the August 2013 issue of … (EVIDENCE) From disturbing statistics such as these, surely it is abundantly clear that Europe-wide legislation is urgently required if we are to eliminate such alarming risks to … (COMMENTARY)

GIVING SOURCES FOR DISCURSIVE WRITING

Earlier in this section, we mentioned the importance of giving your sources for this kind of writing. Naturally, the more professionally you present the resources you have consulted, the more seriously your work will be taken. Bear in mind, too, when you go on to college or university, that setting your sources out correctly will be an important asset. There are several recognised ways of setting out sources. The following one is known as APA style (American Psychological Association) and is commonly used in British academic institutions.

contd

Referencing books

To reference books in the APA style:

> Start with author's name: surname first, then initial. (Followed by the year of publication in brackets) *Then comes the title in italics.* Then the city of publication: and finally the publisher.

A complete book reference should appear like this:

> King, R. (2000) *Brunelleschi's Dome.* London: Penguin.

Referencing newspapers and magazine articles

To reference articles from newspapers or magazines:

> Start with author's name: surname first, then initial. (Followed by the publication date in brackets) Next include the title of the article itself. *Then the name of the publication should come in italics.* And finally the page reference.

A complete article reference should appear like this:

> Goring, R. (2003, January 4) She's Talking Our Language Now. the *Herald.* p. 14.

Electronically sourced material

To reference electronically sourced material:

Name of author (if available) and title of article/publication as you would for a print publication. In place of city of publication and name of publisher, put the web address and the date when the article was posted (if available) and also the date when you accessed.

ONLINE TEST

Check that your knowledge of paragraph structure and referencing is up to scratch online at www.brightredbooks.net/N5English

DON'T FORGET

All references should be arranged in alphabetical order. This should be by the first letter of the author's surname, or by the name of the website if there is no author listed!

ONLINE

For more information on listing web addresses, consult 'APA Lite for College Papers' at www.brightredbooks.net/N5English. See point 6.9 under Web Pages.

THINGS TO DO AND THINK ABOUT

As mentioned previously, there are numerous people against fracking (not least the artist of this cartoon!). Here are some points which opponents might put forward.

- Drilling activities have been known to cause earth tremors.

- Drilling can pollute aquifers (underground channels carrying water).

- Fracking requires great quantities of chemicals. These have to be transported to sites, creating additional pollution.

- In America, firms have not been quick to disclose how they dispose of these chemicals.

- If wells are not properly capped, harmful methane gas may escape, adding to greenhouse-gas worries.

- Increased traffic on roads is not welcome in small communities.

WWW.DAILYMAIL.CO.UK/MAC

'Good news, George. Apparently our gas bills might be a few pence cheaper.'

Either with a partner or on your own, try to compose an introduction to a persuasive essay which is hostile to the idea of fracking. Obviously you will not have space to include all the contrary arguments; but select two key facts to weave into your introduction. First discuss which facts you think would be the most important to include. Give reasons for your final selection.

TRANSACTIONAL WRITING

WHAT IS TRANSACTIONAL WRITING?

Transactional writing uses many of the writing skills we have been discussing in this section. The need is still to produce clear, well-expressed prose, but the information conveyed and the prose style will be adapted to meet certain situation-specific formats. In other words, the layout and the prose style of your transactional writing will vary according to the task your writing is setting out to accomplish. A report has its own particular format and style, as does a book review, a brochure, a process commentary, a set of instructions or a recipe.

In this section, we will look at how to set about a few of these – but, remembering that these are 'real-world' documents, the best model will always be 'real-world' examples of these. So, your research here will need to involve two levels of enquiry:

- obtaining the factual information you wish to communicate
- studying the format of published examples of similar documents.

REPORT-WRITING

Reports are written so that busy people can gather information speedily. The format, accordingly, will reflect this by often offering the reader numbered sections and subheadings to allow them to pinpoint specific information instantly. A basic report could offer the following sections, although, depending on the complexity of the content, these might need to be extended:

1 Introduction – in which you might set out the reasons why the report is needed and an explanation for the selection of these particular sources. Remember, two sources in a report of 1 000 words are sufficient.

2 Findings – in which you set out what was discovered from the sources consulted.

3 Discussion – in which you pull together the information gathered to make clear the implications of these findings (i.e. there is substantial agreement/disagreement, and then spell out focus of the agreement and/or conflict).

4 Conclusion – in which next steps might be suggested on the basis of the findings you have just presented.

These could be further subdivided numerically to cover various aspects of the sections in question:

1 Introduction

   1.1 The purpose of this report is to determine …

   1.2 The sources consulted to arrive at our conclusions were selected to reflect a cross-section of views on …

2 Findings

   2.1 Schools managers appear convinced that the introduction of …

   2.2 Teachers did not appear to share this conviction in that …

   2.3 Pupils were split on the issue, with some …

ONLINE

A useful site for looking at formal reports of this kind is 'The Scottish Government Publications' at www.brightredbooks. net/N5English. Check out carefully the subheading *2020 Routemap for Renewable Energy in Scotland*. As well as being a helpful guide for the structure of your layout, it is a mine of information which could also be valuable for an argumentative or persuasive essay.

REPORT STYLE

Here you need the same writing style you would apply to an argumentative essay:

- Formal, neutral word choice
- Avoidance of figurative/emotive language or informal abbreviations
- Logical progression of information.

The presentation would also benefit from a separate title page in which you give the report's title, the date of presentation and your name. A separate sheet at the end with a precisely documented list of sources would add to your professionalism.

DON'T FORGET

Some of your report information can be conveyed by diagrams, pie charts/ graphs tables or bullet points. Make sure you caption them in a way that makes it clear to the reader why they are there.

REVIEWING

While a report is a highly formal example of transactional writing, a review invites you to give a more personal response. This response may be to a book, a film, a television programme, an art exhibition, a music album, a concert or some other event or happening. This subjectivity allows you a certain flexibility of approach, but always be aware of your reader. It is a good idea to remember that your reader may not have been present or have experienced what you are reviewing, so you must not overlook objective reporting on content as well as personal response to it. You are informing as much as reacting. Here are some pointers for various genres:

DON'T FORGET

A review informs as well as responds. Ensure yours does both.

BOOKS	Title/author/publisher/price
FILMS	Title/director/stars/screening cinema. In some films, the composer, costume or special-effects designer will also play key roles. DVD availability and censor's age-rating need consideration, too.
TV PROGRAMME(S)	Title/director/relevant channel/date of transmission
EXHIBITION/CONCERT	Title/artists involved/location of event/dates
ALBUM	Title/artists/production company/price CD and MP3 download

For books, films and media programmes, make sure you include reference to the genre, setting, **characterisation** and plot before embarking on your review of the success or otherwise of their handling. The style in which you do this can be done formally – as in an argumentative essay – or informally and emotively – as in a persuasive essay. A good guide as to which approach to adopt might be dictated by the seriousness (or otherwise) of the subject matter, no matter which genre from the above grid you choose to review.

ONLINE

For some great book reviews to get you going, check out 'The *Guardian*: Books' at www.brightredbooks.net/ N5English

APPROACHES TO REVIEWING

'Real-world' models for reviews can be found in the weekend sections of many quality newspapers or in weekly/monthly specialist magazines. Before embarking on writing in this genre, it would be wise to study the relevant review section on one of them and to note how professionals deal with objective facts and subjective reactions.

It is probably unlikely that the editor of one of those publications would allow a writer to devote 1000 words to the review of a single book/film/album. It might, therefore, be sensible for you to select two examples on related themes, styles or topics for consideration. A comparison of their relative strengths and weaknesses would be a useful starting point. In the case of novels, those connected by a similar theme – say, love in time of war – would bear profitable exploration.

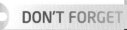

ONLINE TEST

To ensure you have the right idea of how to get started on a piece of transactional writing, test yourself online at www.brightredbooks.net/ N5English

DON'T FORGET

Don't overlook non-fiction books for review. Travel guides, books by celebrity chefs, biographies and 'How to' manuals all offer ample opportunities for comparison of practicality, bias or readability.

 THINGS TO DO AND THINK ABOUT

With transactional writing, no matter the genre, you are entering the world of reality. Make sure you are offering a version of your selected genre which is securely grounded in that world, not in some vague idea of what you think it is. Research the structure and style of the real thing before you start to write.

MANAGING YOUR FOLIO

Writing can be a fairly lonely business. The need for concentration tends to make us want to shut ourselves away to get on with the task. Of course, you will maybe have discussed your choice of folio pieces with a friend or two and will have shown a plan to your teacher. But, once your plan has been approved, you will probably have set about your first draft in some quiet corner of the library or at home, perhaps showing the piece to somebody you know just before handing in the draft.

Now, friends being friends – and catching sight of your neatly typed manuscript – they will probably make polite noises. But what do they *really* think? Seeing clearly that your work is already far advanced, they probably won't tell you in any great critical detail. So, can we really call this peer-reviewing? Is it not more like going through the motions?

FIND A FOLIO FRIEND!

A better method of working might be to find a 'folio friend' *right at the beginning* of the folio-planning process – somebody whose judgement you respect and who knows you and your work fairly well, somebody you see and talk to regularly.

Involve them right from the beginning of the process, not just at its end.

As you discuss possibilities, check with the relevant section of this Study Guide to see how it could help you with the various genres.

START WITH BASICS

Discuss together which genres for the folio you are each contemplating. Go through this Study Guide, looking at the kinds of writing which attract you and in which you may have already shown some ability. How difficult do you think you are going to find an argumentative essay at this level? If you went for that option, what might you choose to write about?

DON'T FORGET ✚

Previewing your intentions is as important as reviewing your outcomes – perhaps even more so.

Maybe you like the idea of personal reflective writing. Maybe you should revisit this territory. Bounce ideas off each other. List potential genres and discuss together the pros and cons of each one. Spend considerable time at this stage before even thinking of a specific title or topic, before planning or drafting a single word. Time well spent at this stage will probably save you a lot of time later on.

RESEARCH TOPICS TOGETHER

So, maybe you have decided on an argumentative essay and prose fiction. Let's look at them, one by one. Very well; so, what controversial topic are you interested in exploring? Discuss together what is involved in gathering evidence. How difficult or easy might this be, given the topic?

Is there any possibility that you could research a topic together, with your friend deciding on a persuasive essay and you an argumentative essay? By pooling your research, you would both become subject 'specialists', with your essays benefiting from the added depth and breadth of joint research.

Use this Study Guide's discursive section to help you try out some approaches to these kinds of writing. Does this kind of writing feel the right choice for you? What do you think? What does your partner think? Consult. Discuss. It's good to air your views, feelings and, yes, doubts at this early stage.

contd

Should you be considering a short story, a similar approach holds good. Is there an idea at the back of your mind? What does your partner make of it? A bit far-fetched? Too complicated for the word limits? Test out your ideas against the suggested processes in the prose section of this book.

TRIANGULATE ADVICE

Teachers have their roles to play in this process also. Once you have discussed your general intentions with your partner and your teacher, the time has probably come to shape up a plan for your teacher's inspection. Once you have the feedback, you are now in the healthy position of having a triple perspective on the plan.

CONSULT REGULARLY

Don't be in any hurry to complete the first draft. Your plan will have broken down the essay into several sections. Consult with your partner at each stage of creating these sections. If you were working on an argumentative essay, the process might go like this:

Introduction

After having checked what this Study Guide has to say about introductions, does your partner feel your introduction is appropriate? Parts missing? Too dull an opening sentence?

Body paragraphs

In a discursive essay, are they sufficient to explore fully your topic? How strong are the opening statements in each section? How convincing is the evidence you are producing? Does your commentary on the evidence do the evidence full justice?

Conclusion

Check again with this book to see if your conclusion matches up with what an examiner might expect. Does your partner agree with how you have rounded off your discussion of this topic? Are there any lingering weaknesses in his/her opinion?

Whatever genres you choose to explore for the folio, adopt a similar approach with your chosen partner for each of your two pieces. Remember, finally, that the examiners are looking for work that reveals appropriate:

- content
- structure
- expression
- technical accuracy

Make sure at this stage that each of these four criteria is being given sufficient attention. You will find that the interchange of ideas with your partner on all these points will strengthen not only your work but your self-confidence, too, as you proceed to the completion of the folio.

CONTINUE THE PROCESS

After your teacher has seen and made suggestions on how the draft might be improved, talk over the proposed changes with your partner. Redraft the local areas that need adjusting.

THINGS TO DO AND THINK ABOUT

In this electronic age, use e-mails to keep in touch with your partner. In this way, changes and improvements can be implemented more quickly and don't need to wait for a face-to-face encounter.

ONLINE

Check out the 'SQA Study Guides' at www.brightredbooks.net/N5English for more useful information on how to manage your time.

ONLINE TEST

Take the 'Managing your Folio' test online at www.brightredbooks.net/N5English

PROOFREADING YOUR FOLIO

In the long process of preparing your drafts, you will likely have made numerous changes: perhaps a missing sentence was added, perhaps you inserted a quotation from a leading authority, or maybe you changed the order of certain paragraphs. This is all to the good. This is how a serious writing process should happen.

But there are hazards, too. As a result of all these improvements, irritating glitches may have crept in while you were concentrating on drafting the major changes. They may seem minor, but nevertheless they count against you in terms of technical accuracy. So, how do we avoid or eliminate them?

LEAVE TIME

Don't leave finalising your 'polished' draft to the last minute. If you allow yourself sufficient time, you can put your essay aside for some time before the due date and come back to it fresh for a final read-through. You will be astonished how many slip-ups you will notice straight away, slip-ups which totally escaped your notice in the white heat of drafting. So, here's another good reason for avoiding brinkmanship.

READ ALOUD

Here's where your folio friend can come in useful again. Reading a text through silently to yourself to check for errors can be unreliable. We tend to 'read' what we *think* we see rather than what is actually on the page. Better still, get your folio friend to read it back to you. He or she is more likely to read what is *actually* there rather than what *you think* is there.

Furthermore, hearing sentences read aloud can often help to detect clumsy expressions or sentences which either go on too long or do not quite make sense.

CHECK LINKAGE

A good essay, whether it be discursive, personal reflective or creative, needs to maintain a smooth flow from beginning to end. The introduction must flow into body paragraphs, and they in turn must run smoothly into each other before merging satisfyingly into your conclusion. Reading aloud will also help here. That clumsy, unprepared-for change of topic will immediately be obvious to the ear when read aloud, although it may have slipped by unnoticed on countless silent readings. There are the basics to demonstrate sequence such as:

Firstly, ...   Furthermore, ...   In addition, ...   What is more, ...   Finally, ...

These show simple progressions from one point in a sequence to the next one. But you may wish to use connectives of transition to move your reader from one topic to quite another:

Now, while it is true to say that ...   As far as ... is concerned, ...   Turning to ... Regarding the question of ...

And, if you want to introduce a brief aside to your reader, there is always; *Incidentally, ...*

If you wish to make a change of direction from a preceding comment, you have various choices:

On the other hand, however, ...   By way of contrast, there is ...   Conversely, ...

SPELL-CHECK

Yes, you've got a spell-check on your computer, but there is only so much it can spot. It will help you out with the more difficult words, but it will not help you when you accidentally type 'bit' when you mean 'but'. Even in university dissertations, examiners constantly complain of finding the following very basic errors. Don't spoil fine work by confusing elementary items like these:

were/we're/where	*who's/whose*
too/to/two	*they're/their/there*
its/it's	*lose/loose*

Better still, go over *now* all the words you know you have been getting wrong in your essays for years. Get them right once and for all! You know which ones I mean!

CHECK PUNCTUATION

From your preparation for Close Reading, you should have a sound knowledge of how punctuation works in creating certain effects. Make sure you apply this knowledge to your own writing. Be particularly careful with direct speech in short stories or personal reflective writing.

WRONG: 'Well, I suppose you've talked to Jean', she sighed.   ✗

CORRECT: 'Well, I suppose you've talked to Jean,' she sighed.   ✓

Above all, avoid the comma splice: the joining-together of two independent statements incorrectly with the use of only a comma.

WRONG: It was a fine spring morning, Hamish decided to go for a walk by the shore.   ✗

CORRECT: It was a fine spring morning. Hamish decided to go for a walk by the shore.   ✓

It being a fine spring morning, Hamish decided to go for a walk by the shore.   ✓

Since it was a fine morning, Hamish decided to go for a walk by the shore.   ✓

A comma will not do the connection! Either use a full stop to acknowledge that these are two independent clauses or statements, or use connecting mechanisms such as the above. If in doubt, consult your teacher. A comma will not do the business here!

CHECK AGREEMENT

In longer sentences, where the subject may have become separated from the rest of the sentence – including the verb – make sure you have not started with a singular subject and ended up with a plural verb, or vice versa.

THINGS TO DO AND THINK ABOUT

Proofreading is the last stage in the long process of getting your folio together. You have put a great deal of work into these two pieces to get this far. You just cannot let yourself down by failing to spot typos, spelling errors, awkward expressions or ill-considered punctuation. These may have been spotted at an earlier stage but, with cutting and pasting, you may have let them slip back in. It can happen. Ensure that it doesn't!

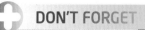

DON'T FORGET

You have had plenty of time to prepare your folio pieces. So, imagine the poor impression you give of yourself to the examiner if you leave spelling mistakes or typos in your final version.

ONLINE

For more resources on proofreading, click the 'BBC Skillswise: Editing and Proofreading' link at www.brightredbooks.net/N5English

ONLINE TEST

Take the 'Proofreading your Folio' test online at www.brightredbooks.net/N5English

PREPARING FOR THE EXAM

Exam preparation is not an event; it is a process. It is a process which needs to begin a long time before the big day. It is a process which requires you to do a reasonable amount of work on a regular basis, rather than a lot of work hectically at the last minute. This latter approach is of greatly inferior value. Ideally, set yourself a revision timetable which begins well in advance of the exam date. Yes, you have regular homework to contend with as well, but set aside time in addition to this which will help you to get ahead. This is so that, as you approach the exam, you do so with the quiet confidence of knowing you are really well prepared. That is about the only thing that will quell those butterflies in your stomach as you go into the exam room.

ORGANISE YOUR TIME

First of all, jot down a list of the revision areas you need to prepare. For National 5 English, you will need to consider your notes on Close Reading (which will also serve you well with your Scottish Context): word choice, sentence structure, punctuation, figurative language, summarising and inference – in other words, all the notes you have put together from your work on Chapter 2 of this book.

Then there's the critical essay to consider; not just your structuring advice to be mastered (which you read about in Chapter 3) but also the text(s) for your critical essay and Scottish literature. How often have you read them in your own time in order to say you really *know* them? And how about those quotations your teacher suggested were key to writing about characters and themes? How readily can you summon them up? And how about some time to write a practice essay once you are on top of your essay-writing skills and text(s)? Quite a lot to be fitted in; hence the need for a revision timetable.

SET A TIMETABLE

Nobody knows better about your homework/study commitments than you, so you yourself will need to draw up your own personal time lines. For some people, two hours a night may well be enough; others may manage a little more. What is important, however, is that you *do* have some kind of study timetable which takes account of other subjects as well as English, of course. Make it realistic; allow yourself breaks for cups of coffee and evenings when you are free to relax properly. You may moan a bit, but just think about how success in this exam will allow you to move on next year.

Here is just a suggestion of what a revision timetable *might* look like. Adapt it to suit your own circumstances. Foreground the areas which you think need most work. No two study timetables will ever look alike.

H = Homework   OR = Other subject revision

ECR = English Close Reading revision   EQ = quotations

ET = English/Scottish text(s) revision   EEP = English essay practice

Day	6:00–6:30	6:45–7:45	8:00–8:45	9:00–9:30
Monday	H	H	ECR	OR
Tuesday	OR	OR	H	Free
Wednesday	OR	OR	ET	OR
Thursday	H	OR	OR	ECR
Friday	EQ	OR	Free	Free
Saturday	Free	Free	Free	Free
Sunday	OR	EEP	ET	H

DON'T FORGET

A little revision regularly will pay greater benefits than a lot at the last minute.

ONLINE

For more help with planning a revision timetable, click on the 'Get Revising: Timetable' link at www.brightredbooks.net/N5English

DON'T FORGET

Set a timetable – and stick to it! Give a copy to somebody else at home, so that they know you really *are* working hard. And maybe they'll give you a friendly nudge from time to time …?

CONSIDER A STUDY BUDDY

Some people can only revise when they are shut away in peace and quiet and left totally on their own. Some people thrive on the encouragement of revising with a study buddy. If you are one of these people, find someone with whom you get on well, one who has the same exam commitments as yourself. Then synchronise your revision timetables so that you both come prepared for the session.

So, one evening it might be targeted areas from your Close Reading notes – for example, sentence structure/punctuation/tone. 'Tell me five things you might consider saying about sentence structure.' Or 'How might emotive tone reveal itself?' Then work your way through your notes, separating them into manageable chunks as you go along. Take turns to ask the questions.

Another evening, you might want to check how well you know your quotations. '*I will fall like a* ... is the start of the quotation. How does it finish?' Then you might want to check your detailed knowledge of, say, an act of a play or the development of a certain character. 'What are the main events of Act 2?', or 'How does John Hale change in the course of *The Crucible*? Have you got quotations to back up what you are saying about these changes?'

The very fact of working out the areas which you both feel you need to target – and then setting a timetable for so doing – can make you feel a great deal better about yourselves and your chances of success. Try mapping out a study programme to suit individual needs.

 **THINGS TO DO AND THINK ABOUT**

A wise man once remarked:

Success is the sum of small efforts, repeated day in and day out.

Clearly, he knew about revising for National 5!

THE MANDATORY UNITS

SO, HOW DO THESE UNITS OPERATE?

They will be assessed by your teachers or lecturers, who will be devising their own assessment programmes. They enjoy considerable flexibility in how they conduct these assessments to give maximum variety and interest to the assessment process. Knowing your abilities first-hand, they will decide the most appropriate ways to generate convincing evidence of your performance. At times, they will be able to assess several outcomes at once; at others, you will be given discrete tasks to perform, whereby one skill will be assessed individually. These Units fall into two areas: Analysis and Evaluation and Creation and Production.

ANALYSIS AND EVALUATION

In this Unit, you will be expected to point to evidence of two successful outcomes:

Outcome 1

Understand, analyse and evaluate detailed **written texts** by explaining the purposes and audience; identify and explain the main ideas and supporting details; apply knowledge and understanding of language to explain meaning and effect, using appropriate critical terminology.

This may sound somewhat daunting – but it is basically extending your Close Reading skills to encompass certain other skills.

Outcome 2

Understand, analyse and evaluate detailed **spoken language** by identifying and explaining the purpose and audience, identifying and explaining the main ideas and supporting details and applying knowledge and understanding of language to explain meaning and effect.

Again, this may sound quite complicated – but this book takes you step by step through the process of learning to listen to spoken language and will help you deal with its various purposes and challenges.

CREATION AND PRODUCTION

In this Unit, you will be expected to point to evidence of two successful outcomes:

Outcome 1

Create and produce detailed **written texts** by selecting significant ideas and content, using a format and structure appropriate to the purpose and audience, applying knowledge and understanding of language in terms of language choice and technical accuracy, and communicating meaning at first reading.

The aim here is competent essay-writing, respecting the expectations of various genres.

Outcome 2

Take part in detailed **spoken interactions** by selecting significant ideas and content, using a format and structure appropriate to the purpose and audience, applying knowledge and understanding of language in terms of language choice, communicating meaning at a first hearing, and using significant aspects of non-verbal communication.

Again, at first reading, this may sound pretty fearsome – but this book helps you to take part successfully in group interaction and to interpret listening activities in a way that makes clear what the intentions of the original communication were and for what kind of audience it was intended.

GLOSSARY OF CRITICAL TERMS

At this stage of your studies, you need to be able to use the professional vocabulary of criticism to maximise the impact of your comments in spoken and written work. The following list is by no means comprehensive, but it gives you some of the more common terms to add to your critical vocabulary.

Alliteration

The repetition of a particular consonant – or consonant sound – at the beginning of a group of words to create a certain sound effect. *Cold clay clads his coffin.* Here the harsh sound of the letter 'c' matches the grimness of the description. *Soft sighing of the southern seas.* Here the soft 's' sound mimics the gentleness of the water's sound.

Anecdote

A brief story, often encountered in Close Reading passages, to illustrate a point.

Anti-climax

Often encountered when the final item in a list is the least important or oddly out of place. In Close Reading work, the effect is usually to add humour.

Assonance

The repetition of a certain group of similar-sounding vowels in words close to each other, again used to create a certain aural effect. *And murmuring of innumerable bees.* Assonance is to vowels what alliteration is to consonants.

Characterisation

The building-up and establishing of convincing character portrayals through means such as dialogue, actions or the reaction of others to the character in question.

Connotation

The associations we carry around in our minds – often unthinkingly – about certain words. For example, we associate 'dove' with peace, or 'rose' with love. Alternatively, verbs like 'cling' suggest an insecure, dependent frame of mind, while 'skip' suggests a light-hearted mood. Referring to connotations is often very useful for dealing with word choice or imagery questions in Close Reading.

Context

In Close Reading work, you may be asked to suggest how the context helps you to understand the meaning of a word. The context is the surrounding sentence or paragraph in which the word appears.

Denotation

Usually discussed in association with connotation. It is the dictionary definition of a word or term, free of the associations we have with connotations.

Ellipsis

In mid-sentence, these three dots can be used to suggest an interruption, hesitation or indecision. Used at the end of the sentence, they can suggest anticipation or suspense. *The door opened and a hand appeared ...*

Enjambment

In poetry, this is the running-on of one line into another or into several others, either to give a conversational feel to the content or sometimes to suggest a speeding-up for an effect of urgency. It can also make the reader wait for a key point to be made when the sentence finally stops.
... for my purpose holds
To sail beyond the sunset, and the baths
Of all the western stars, until I die.

Figurative language

This is language which uses figures of speech such as similes, metaphors or personification to create pictures ('figures') in our minds to make descriptions more vivid and graphic. It will often turn up in Close Reading work and literature study. Useful, too, in persuasive writing.

Foreshadow

Useful term for your critical essays or context work. A fairly minor event or incident can be said to 'foreshadow' a much more important one later in the text. It prepares the reader for a more significant event so that the later one is not wholly unexpected. For example, a mildly aggressive action can suggest a more violent one to come.

Genre

This is the type, or category, of literature: poetry, drama or prose. Genre also categorises the type of writing you may select for your Folio – discursive or creative being the main genres here.

Hyperbole

This is the technical literary name for exaggeration. It is often used to create a certain effect (often humorous) or to emphasise something. *The list goes on for miles. He never fails to get lost. I've seen more fat on a chip.* Hyperbole often turns up in tone questions in Close Reading. Can also be useful in persuasive writing.

Image/imagery

A device used to create a picture ('image') in the mind which exploits the connotations of a word to give it greater impact on the reader. Frequently at the core of questions in Close Reading work. Understanding of the working of imagery is also very necessary for commenting on literature and in your own creative writing where you wish to make a point with graphic vividness.

Irony

Often saying the opposite of what you mean. *The concert lasts four hours? With no interval? Wonderful!* Used frequently in questions of tone in Close Reading to criticise or mock something or somebody in a humorous or bitter way to make a critical point. Useful, too, in persuasive writing.

Literal/literally

Used when you want a word or phrase to mean exactly what it says, as opposed to being 'metaphorical' in its use, where the meaning is more figurative. For example, *My teacher went through the roof* is metaphorical, suggesting simply the anger of your teacher. If the phrase were used literally, it would suggest that your teacher did structural damage to the building.

Litotes

This is the opposite of hyperbole (see above), whereby something is understated rather than exaggerated, often for humorous effect. *Hamish is not the sharpest knife in the drawer* suggests that the intelligence of Hamish is somewhat limited.

Metaphor

This is a literary device whereby two items are compared. They are not, as in a simile, *like* each other; one *becomes* the other. *You're an angel. He was rocked by a tsunami of self-pity.*

Onomatopoeia

Here the sound of the word mimics and thereby gives a clue to its meaning. *Clink, fizz, rip, honk, boom, purr* are all words which suggest their meaning in their sound. *Bubbles gargled delicately* is an example of this used for aural effect by Seamus Heaney, suggesting a sound picture of the noise of bubbles emerging gently from mud at the bottom of a pond.

Oxymoron

The placing side by side of two words which appear to contradict each other, in order to startle and to create a vivid impact on the reader. *A deafening silence. A wise fool.*

Paradox

This is a form of extended oxymoron in which seemingly contradictory ideas are placed side by side. *The child is father of the man.* Its aim, like that of the oxymoron, is to arrest the reader's attention by its startling and, at first glance, puzzling nature.

Parallel structure

These are patterns of either phrases or words which give a pleasing predictability and rhythm to the sentence. The effect is to add emphasis to what is being said. *It is by logic we prove, but by intuition we discover* (da Vinci). *The ants were everywhere:* climbing *over jampots,* swarming *under the sink,* scrambling *into cupboards,* diving *into the bin.* The likeness of pattern here (preposition, noun, verb) makes for a more memorable phrase and creates a greater impact than a less patterned structure would.

Parenthesis

A parenthesis can be found between two dashes, two brackets or two commas. It is a phrase which adds interesting additional, but not essential, information to what is being discussed. It is often targeted by examiners in sentence-structure questions in Close Reading.

Personification

Personification is when an inanimate object is given living qualities. *The sun caressed her back. Hunger stalked the land.*

Repetition

This may take the form of repeated words or phrases to underline/intensify the idea the writer is seeking to emphasise at a particular point. *A good cyclist needs … A good cyclist hopes that … But a good cyclist knows above all that …* Note that these repetitions in the closing stages of a text might be building to a climax. Sentence-structure questions in Close Reading work may focus on this device.

Rhetorical question

These are questions expecting no direct answer, rather the reader's support for the writer's views. *Who wants to see a child suffer in this way?* Here the reader is expected to share the writer's horror at the ill-treatment of children.

Rhyme

The pairing of words with the same sound, used usually at the ends of lines in poetry:
On either side the river lie
Long fields of barley and of rye.
In more modern poetry, poets may attempt what is called a half-rhyme:
When have I last looked on
The round green eyes and the long wavering bodies
Of the dark leopards of the moon?
All the wild witches, those most noble ladies.

Here the words *on/moon* and *bodies/ladies* are related but not identical in sound, thus targeting aural cohesion but avoiding undue attention to rhyming words.

Rhythm

The pulse felt within a line of poetry, created through alternating unstressed and stressed syllables. *On either side the river lie …* or, alternatively, stressed and unstressed: *Willows whiten, aspens quiver.*

Sarcasm

Frequently expressed by uttering the opposite of what is meant. *My good friend, the traffic warden.* Be alert for this in tone questions in Close Reading work. You can also use it to good effect in your own persuasive writing.

Simile

One of the most common devices found in figurative language. It is a comparison between two items using 'like' or 'as': '*As idle as a painted ship upon a painted ocean*'. Used to bring the comparison vividly alive in the mind's eye.

Stanza

This is a means of referring to formal units in a poem, often when the units are of unequal length. For example, a Petrarchan sonnet has two stanzas: an octet followed by a sestet.

Style

This is a reference to how a writer creates effects in his or her work by, say, imagery, word choice, tone, anecdote, sentence structure or any other features which help to mark out the distinctive signature of that particular author or passage.

Symbolism

This is an item or action which stands for more than itself in a novel or poem. For example, a character might be seen to be pulling the petals off a flower, suggesting some later act of violence of a more serious nature.

Synonym

An alternative word for the same thing. Vital for success in understanding questions in Close Reading.

Theme

A central idea that binds together characters or situations in a novel or short story. It is what the text is *about*. For instance, the theme of the dangers of false appearance is everywhere you look in *Macbeth*. The Macbeths exploit it, as do the witches. Other people such as Duncan become its victim, as, ultimately, do the Macbeths themselves.

Tone

This is the unspoken attitude of writers to their subject. In Close Reading work, you are expected to tease this out by looking for internal clues such as hyperbole, emotive language or colloquial language.

Word choice

In Close Reading, this is one of the more common questions you will encounter. You need to select words from the text which appear to you to identify an effect or a tone that the writer is attempting to convey. For instance, does he/she refer to a woman as 'slim' or 'scrawny'? The word chosen will indicate his/her attitude to the woman in question, i.e. elegant and trim, or underweight to the point of being unattractive.